Personal Branding
MASTERY
For Entrepreneurs

Personal Branding
MASTERY
For Entrepreneurs

Chris J.Reed

International #1 Best Seller

in 4 Countries in 17 Categories

and #1 in 19 Hot New Release Categories

Top 100 Book on Amazon Canada (Ranked #53)

For Your Book Bonus Visit:

https://personalmasterybook.com/bookbonus

LinkedIn: www.linkedin.com/in/b2bsocialmarketing

Author Website: www.chrisjreed.com

Website: www.thedarkartofmarketing.com

Email: chris@blackmarketing.com

Mobile/Whatsapp: (+65)9026 1966

Skype: BlackMarketingGlobal

WeChat: LinkedInMarketing

1st Edition 2017

First Published in 2017 for Chris J Reed by Evolve Global Publishing

PO Box 327 Stanhope Gardens NSW 2768 info@evolveglobalpublishing.com

www.evolveglobalpublishing.com

Book Layout: © 2017 Evolve Global Publishing

ISBN: (Paperback)   978-1-64008-217-5 (Ingram)

ISBN: (Hardcover) 978-1-64136-719-6 (Ingram)

ISBN-13: (Createspace): 978-1975868956

ISBN-10: (Createspace): 1975868951

ISBN: (Smashwords) 9781370713479

ASIN: (Amazon Kindle): B073ZLJ89V

This book is available on Barnes & Noble, Kobo, Apple iBooks (digital), and Google Books (digital).

Personal Branding
MASTERY
For Entrepreneurs

On Audiobooks

Available from:

Or Visit www.chrisjreed.com

Dedication

This book is dedicated to Chester Bennington, lead singer and creator of Linkin Park and the Linkin Park sound—my saviour, my inspiration, my energy, my anger, my angst, my feelings. You expressed things that I never could. Life won't be the same without you. You are my inspiration for my personal brand.

Table of Contents

About the Author

Chris J. Reed is a two-time #1 international best-selling author and popular public speaker who has maintained his status as one of the world's most viewed LinkedIn profiles.

Chris's own personal branding is 'The only NASDAQ-listed CEO with a Mohawk!'

He is now a serial global entrepreneur after founding Black Marketing—Enabling LinkedIn for You (a NASDAQ- listed, award-winning plc) and The Dark Art of Marketing—Personal Branding for Entrepreneurs. Black Marketing provides worldwide marketing services to entrepreneurs from its Singapore headquarters.

Chris has been named an Official LinkedIn Power Profile every year between 2012 and 2017, and he is the only marketing entrepreneur to win this title every year since the award's inception. In addition, Chris has one of the world's most viewed LinkedIn profiles, with 55,000 followers; he is recognised as one of the region's top social sellers, and he is also one of the world's top 100 bloggers on LinkedIn.

Chris won the Social Media Entrepreneur of the Year 2017 Award by CMO Asia/World Brand Congress as well as Asia's Most Influential Digital Media Professional also by CMO Asia. Black Marketing is an award-winning business: It won the Social Media Marketing Award, by *Singapore Business Review* and the British Chamber of Commerce Singapore Small Business Rising Star, and it has been nominated for The Agency of the Year by *Marketing Magazine* and Social Media Influencer of the Year.

Chris is also a vastly experienced event speaker and chairperson. He happily speaks and chairs at conferences and company events, and he regularly holds LinkedIn workshops. He lectures about LinkedIn and personal branding at the the Chinese University of Hong Kong Business School.

Chris is also the chair of the British Chamber of Commerce Singapore Marketing and Creative Business Group, the most active group at the chamber, and he is an elected board member of the BritCham, Singapore.

Chris mentors for the CMO Council-Singapore Management University Business School and National University of Singapore students.

Chris's late grandfather always told him: 'It is not what you know, it is who you know', and LinkedIn has proved him right.

Introduction

From the #1 international best-selling author Chris J. Reed, 'the only NASDAQ-listed CEO with a Mohawk!', comes his new book, *Personal Branding Mastery for Entrepreneurs.*

In it, Chris will tell you all about how you, as an entrepreneur, can develop your personal brand beyond LinkedIn. You are an entrepreneur, and your personal brand is what everyone is buying into.

Your clients, your shareholders, your employees, your partners, the media . . . future clients, employees, investors . . . they are all buying into the power and values of your personal brand.

That's why you need to start working on it now. In this new book, Chris will talk from his own personal experience about how he created a personal brand from nothing and knowing no one when he left the UK and came to Singapore to become an Asian entrepreneur.

Chris will explain how he became 'the only NASDAQ-listed CEO with a Mohawk!' and how this personal brand has transformed his businesses. Chris covers all aspects of personal branding for entrepreneurs, including what it is, why you should have it, his personal brand story, the ups and downs of having a personal brand, and why you need to be more American and less English or Asian in your personal branding.

Chris will also cover what elements of his disruptive DNA have enabled him to accentuate his own personal brand in his entrepreneurial journey. Chris also covers how LinkedIn is the foundation for your personal brand and emphasises that it should also be communicated everywhere else from your YouTube to your Wikipedia, your thought leadership outside of LinkedIn, to winning awards, getting up on stage and speaking, to having your own book.

Chris will discuss how your dress and look impact your personal brand, both positively and negatively, why great entrepreneurs like

Richard Branson, Elon Musk, Steve Jobs, and Bill Gates all have great but divisive personal brands, and he explains why their respective companies would be nothing without their personal branding.

Chris will also discuss David Beckham, Gareth Emery, and Prince, and what made their personal brands so effective and influential in succeeding in what they have done.

Chris will share personal branding tips from the Joker, *Breaking Bad*, Darth Vader, *American Psycho*, and *The Godfather*, which you can put into practice yourself to enhance your own personal brand.

This new book, *Personal Branding Mastery for Entrepreneurs*, will give all the tips, lessons, and help that you need as an entrepreneur to create, manage, and enhance your own personal brand to enable you to achieve all of your professional objectives.

Chapter One

What Is Personal Branding?

Personal branding is everything about LinkedIn. LinkedIn is a peer-to-peer network in a business context: It's all about personal branding. Your personal brand is what your brand values are.

So, if you are an FMCG brand, like Coca-Cola, or a brand like McKinsey or a brand like Singtel, and then you look at the brand values, you will decipher their brand from their design, from things like the Mohawk, things like the hair, things like the colour black, and things like what the company stands for. Since it is a peer-to-peer network, LinkedIn is all about people.

10 Questions about Executive Branding

1. **Tell us about yourself and what you do.** I am the CEO and Founder of Black Marketing, enabling LinkedIn for you.

2. **What is executive branding?** Executive branding is all about you and your personal brand, developing your personal brand to promote you and your company.

3. **Why do individuals need it?** You are a personal brand, just like Nike is a personal brand, or like Apple. So, think about your personal brand and brand values, just like those brands.

4. **How do companies benefit from executive branding?** Executive branding is all about the CEO, the leader of it, and the people within it developing their personal brand to promote the

company. The company benefits because the leader and CEO, the CMO, and the people within it are using branding and using their own executive branding to promote their company. So, the company benefits overall.

5. **What are three elements of a great executive brand?** The first one is style. You have to have something that really stands out, for example a Mohawk or a beard or a moustache, or something really cool or interesting, or the way you dress, the way you look, and what you say. The second is your thought leadership: be provocative, be interesting, be controversial, but never be boring. Look at how you come across, look at how you communicate. The third is choose the platform. It could be LinkedIn, it could be Twitter, it could be Instagram, but ensure you choose your platform to communicate your personal brand.

6. **Can you name two people who function as brands?** Richard Branson is the most notable one on LinkedIn. He has 10 million followers. He has nailed it to a T. Look at his pictures, look at his thought leadership. It's amazing. Then there's Candice Galek who is absolutely amazing. She is the number one profile on LinkedIn, even though she only has 40,000 connections on LinkedIn compared with Richard Branson's 10 million, but she has been marketing herself and marketing Bikini Luxe through her thought leadership, through her personal brand. She has generated an enormous amount of money, and she has a great physical presence in terms of driving people to Bikiniluxe.com through personal branding and through thought leadership on LinkedIn.

7. **Why aren't more executives in Asia learning personal branding?** It is what I call the 'be less English and be more American' scenario. Lots of English people and lots of Asian people want to be modest. They don't want to tell people about themselves. They think it is over-promoting and over-publicising, but it is actually the only way that people find out about you. So,

go somewhere in between: Don't be too American, but don't be too English. Go somewhere in the middle and talk about your achievements, and people will relate to that. People like success. In Asia in particular, people like success.

8. **What are the first steps towards creating your personal brand?** Look at your brand values and analyse yourself, just as you would another brand. Whether it is H & M, whether it is Uniqlo, or whether it is NASDAQ, regardless, it's a brand. So, look at the brand values of you, just like you look at the brand values of someone like Apple or Nike. Identify your brand values, and then disseminate and promote positive brand values.

9. **What is the best platform to showcase your personal brand?** Obviously, I am going to say LinkedIn. LinkedIn is obviously number one by far from a professional point of view. There are 500 million business people who are all on there, and these people are all engaging with each other on a professional basis. They give you the same amount of space as Richard Branson. You can have the same amount of space as Candice Galek. You can be the next Candice Galek because you can promote yourself on LinkedIn better than anywhere else in the world in a professional context, and that is why it beats Facebook or Twitter, which are not professional. LinkedIn is professional and you're professional, so be on LinkedIn.

10. **What are the three most important things on your LinkedIn profile?** Obviously the first is the picture. You have to have the picture to show the Mohawk. The Mohawk is the USP, but then you have to have a nice strap-line. The strap-line has to create an awareness of what you actually do. At the moment my strap-line is that I am the only CEO listed on NASDAQ with a Mohawk, let alone working in Asia and doing LinkedIn through our company, Black Marketing. Then, you have to look at your summary section. Your summary section describes you as a person. It's your brand values. Put in things there that

are interesting and that are not just about your company, but your journey. What have you done? What are your successes? What have you learned and what are you actually adding to communities? Why should people look at you? Why should people talk to you? So, it is your photograph, your strap-line, and your summary section.

Chapter Two

Why Have a Personal Brand?

If you're an entrepreneur, people are buying into you, just like they're buying into me in my work. It's all about your personal brand: You have to elevate and communicate your brand values, just like you would do with another brand, like Coca-Cola or Nike. Strap-lines, like 'I think different', or 'Just do it!', are powerful tools used in personal branding.

LinkedIn is your first port of call because it's your foundation for when people find you on Google as it's the first thing that comes up. People then click on your LinkedIn profile, and a positive or negative impression is gained through it. So we'll start there and use that as a platform to accentuate your holistic personal branding strategy.

The power of LinkedIn is that you can really position yourself: On LinkedIn, you broadcast your strap-line, add your values in the summary section, talk about your journey, share your successes, discuss your failures, and review what you've learnt. One of the mistakes some people make is that they just talk about their job. Instead, when you are on LinkedIn, imagine yourself at a networking event and think about what you would do to enhance your reputation and share your personality with somebody else.

Talk about the facets of your business that are of interest to your target audience. Identify common interests and then open up a dialogue to discuss this common ground: This is what you're doing when you publicise your brand values, and that's what you do with your personal branding. You look at the values you have, then explore how you can enhance and talk about these values in a way that people actually respect, endorse, and subscribe to your message.

LinkedIn is all about personal branding within a peer-to-peer network and in a business context. It is the ideal platform to publicise your personal branding and your brand values. So, for instance, you might look at brands like Coca-Cola. Then, you identify the brand values, and then you decide how to brand these values through design, like the use of colours, images, and text. This process also involves identifying what the company stands for, including the brand values of the company, which also reflects on you. This process is critical because LinkedIn is a peer support network. It's all about people.

There are only 17 pages on LinkedIn that have more than a million followers because people follow people. People engage with people via other people. So, enhancing your personal brand is extraordinarily important: Public speaking, which I do three times per week, chairing conferences, chairing events, and putting yourself out there in terms of thought leadership via blogging and creating content ensures that your brand is seen and later recognised. Make sure your personal brand is being enhanced as a result of it. You're investing in your personal brand, giving up a brand association with other people, and you're building your personal brand via other people engaging with you.

I have a LinkedIn power profile because I spend an enormous amount of time investing in how I use LinkedIn. My following is large because I apply the principles of social selling. I have one of the most viewed profiles in the world because I'm using unique content in my personal brand: People love the Mohawk.

In Singapore, I walk into a bar or restaurant, and people recognise me from LinkedIn. It's distinctive because other people aren't wearing this hairstyle. It's both interesting and important that something unique is more compelling from a personal branding point of view.

Your personal brand is what's going to sell your business on LinkedIn. Your personal brand will sell you as an entrepreneur, your personal brand will find you investors, and it will make or break your company. It's all about employer branding as an entrepreneur.

It's what I call the Richard Branson effect. People want to work for Virgin, and they respect Virgin because of Richard Branson. Imagine where Virgin would be without Richard Branson. Nowhere. Personal branding starts at the top; it starts with the CEO, and it is just as applicable for CEOs of multinational companies as it is for entrepreneurs and for founders, like you and me. Personal branding is essential to achieve our goals, and it is something that you can achieve yourself on LinkedIn by applying the tips in this book.

Chapter Three

The Power of Personal Branding on LinkedIn

Speaker 1: Good morning everyone and welcome to Link'd AM. I've got a guest on today, Chris Reed.

Chris Reed: Hi.

Speaker 1: Chris, well, according to his LinkedIn profile, it says Chris Mohawk Reed. I wonder why? Chris and I used to work together in Manchester. Of course, Chris is the CEO of Black Marketing. It's a marketing consultancy. Hi, Chris. How are you doing? Thanks for joining us.

Chris Reed: Pleasure.

Speaker 1: You've been named, what? LinkedIn Power Profile for the past . . . How many years is it now?

Chris Reed: Six years.

Speaker 1: Six years. Wow, and 70,000 followers. My goodness.

Chris Reed: Yup.

Speaker 1: That's amazing. We're going to be talking about tactics. The book that you wrote, which is a number one international seller, what was it called? LinkedIn Mastery for Entrepreneurs?

Chris Reed: Entrepreneurs. Yup, that's the one.

Speaker 1: So, explain what's behind that.

Chris Reed: The idea behind that is because I write blogs all the time, obviously on LinkedIn, but I wanted to produce a book that encapsulated all the blogs, all the advice over the last few years that

I'd learned by putting into practice personal branding, employer branding, social selling, thought leadership, and content marketing, then condense it all into a book.

We literally did this in about 12 weeks, and then launched it on Amazon, so it became number one on Amazon.com in Canada, in the US, in the UK, in Australia, in Europe. So, it became just phenomenal.

Even now, people are still buying it, and people are downloading it. I give it away to people when I meet them for presentations or for talks and so forth. People just love it because it encapsulates everything you should do on LinkedIn in a simple book.

Speaker 1: That's interesting because I think a lot of people still think of LinkedIn as a place where you're just going to go to find a job. That's not the case; is it? LinkedIn isn't all about that at all.

Chris Reed: No. It has changed dramatically over the last four or five years, and it has now become a social selling platform. It enables you to not only find the employer that you want to be employed by, but more importantly, you can find a client.

From an entrepreneurial point of view, I can go and find a client by using the data on LinkedIn anywhere in the world. We have clients across the world, even in Shanghai, in Singapore, in Hong Kong, in Sydney, in Europe, and in America. Because it's LinkedIn, I can find that person on my team, I can find that person anywhere.

It's very much a social selling platform, a sales and marketing platform, but also it's now a thought leadership platform. It is now the biggest publishing platform in the world through the Pulse. So, anyone can write a blog, and we do this a lot for our clients: create blogs, create thought leadership, and enable them to be thought leaders and use content marketing to also drive business.

If I put content out there, I get someone to react to me on LinkedIn. I then follow up with a conversation. It's classic social selling. I am doing the reacting because they're doing the pushing, in effect. They're already approaching me, they're viewing my profile and engaging with my content. Then, I have a conversation with them about how you use LinkedIn.

So, I am literally using content to drive my business. I'm using the Sales Navigator platform on LinkedIn to drive my business. The one thing we don't really use it for is the one thing that it's famous for, which is the recruitment side of things. I mean, we do when we do our recruitment, but that's not what we do.

Ninety five percent of what we do is thought leadership and social selling.

Speaker 1: One of the things that I really like is that you talk about LinkedIn as a business network event. That's how you should treat it. You say there's eight reasons why it's like a business networking event. Can you touch on a couple of those?

Chris Reed: Sure. Basically, you go to a business event: What's the first thing you do? You approach people who look welcoming. You approach people that look nice and friendly, so you look at their picture. That's what LinkedIn's about. You look at someone's picture. If you don't like someone's picture on LinkedIn, or they don't have a picture, you don't tend to approach them.

Speaker 1: That's where the Mohawk comes in.

Chris Reed: Precisely; that's my branding. But it's a point of difference. I was at a gallery event last night in Shanghai. In Shanghai, I got approached by one person who said, 'I've never met you before, but we connected on LinkedIn, and I recognised you from your LinkedIn picture'.

Speaker 1: Very good.

Chris Reed: I mean, how phenomenal is that? In the middle of a gallery with 10,000 people there. In the middle of Shanghai, 20 or 30 million people, just phenomenal. I get that quite a lot because people are always saying, 'Yeah, I recognise you because of your Mohawk', so it's part of personal branding, but it's also an icebreaker.

People immediately say, 'You have this Mohawk. Why do you have the Mohawk? How does that actually work?' It's all about networking but making it interesting. The summary section on LinkedIn must be in the first person. It must be interesting. That's about your career but not just about your current job.

Because what's the first thing people do when they go to a networking event? They say, 'What did you do?' Alternatively, they say, 'How did you come Asia?' I will reply, 'Oh, I came to Asia because of X, Y, and Z. I used to work at Manchester with Carl and I went here, and then I went there, then I went there'.

You tell the other person about your career and about your story because that's what people like to hear: stories. That's your summary section. Then, your experiences are obviously about what you do now and what you can do for them.

It isn't just about what you do at that moment, but what you can do for somebody else. That's what I mean: It's networking. Because the whole thing about LinkedIn is that it's a catalyst to meet people.

Speaker 1: I love that because one of the things that I've always seen on LinkedIn is that people talk about different experiences, but they don't really go into that story as you say. They don't tell that story. The other thing that really jumped out at me is that you don't hard sell, but you social sell. What does that mean?

Chris Reed: Well, it's very much about things like using content. I put content out there, and then someone reacts to my content. They like it, they share it, they engage, they comment. I then approach them and build a relationship. It's like you're networking. By the time you've met someone in a networking event the second or third time, you feel much more comfortable with each other.

It's all about trust or relationship-building. It's social. That's what LinkedIn's about. I've met some fantastic people on LinkedIn by sharing content, and they have shared my content. I have liked them, they've liked me. I've commented, they've commented. You build relationships. Then, you feel much more comfortable about saying, 'Oh by the way, this is the service we do. Do you want to have a chat about what we can do for you, and vice versa?'

It's all about using things like content and contributing to the conversation that enables you to then have that selling discussion or not. It could be that they just like and comment on your stuff, and their connections see your content.

It becomes social that way. They introduce you to some of the people they know. That's what I mean about social selling. It's all about using the social skills you have, the networking process on LinkedIn, and how well my book is doing on Amazon.com, because it associates us with the business world.

People like unique, visual things on LinkedIn. You want to share, comment, and like. I recorded a talk I did in Shanghai, for example, and I shared it on LinkedIn. People liked it and shared it.

Shanghai Airport does a really good job in terms of employer branding. They're developing and refining their branding, talking to employees, and talking about their staff. If you do personal branding, content marketing, and company branding, you need to then message people to find that job or find that investment or find that client.

You can do all of this on LinkedIn. There are 11 different ways to go about doing this on LinkedIn. The first one is invitations. You can use invitations to send to people you're not connected with. There's a loophole in LinkedIn that allows you to message people for free using an invitation.

In some ways, LinkedIn is very much a gamification platform. The more you do, the more you get out it. If you go and develop your personal brand, your content marketing strategy, your company page, and you get your messaging right, you too can achieve all your goals and you too can head the rankings amongst professionals like you on LinkedIn.

Speaker 1: I am very convinced. Okay; I have a question.

Chris Reed: Yeah.

Speaker 1: What would be a good approach to make the first few connections on LinkedIn?

Chris Reed: Basically, you reach out to people who you think may be useful to you and your career in terms of being an entrepreneur. LinkedIn is very much about your business portals and your business feed, so you get a lot of interesting people sharing interesting things about business.

It could be a business in Singapore, a business in Asia, businesses in the whole of Asia Pacific, or the world. There's always a blog on there about reading books, blogs that talk about which books CEOs are reading, and how you can get inspired by reading a book. It's all encouraging.

The process is really all about embracing the world of LinkedIn through personalities in a business context. It's key. It's very hard to find that anywhere else in the world. It's about who you know, not what you know. It's about reaching out and using those contacts, but also using those contacts' experience.

Then, you come up with ideas and identify niches in the market of your industry. Then, you create your own business, but you can't do that if you know nothing about the business world. You must build your knowledge about the business world. So, the take-home message is that you need to seize all the opportunities on LinkedIn to learn about the business world and then go for it.

Chapter Four

My Personal Branding Story

My personal brand journey started in Singapore and moved onward and upward based on the work that I have done building businesses (my own and other people's), my LinkedIn workshops, speaking engagements, being a Power Profile on LinkedIn for six consecutive years, writing a best-selling book, and floating a company on NASDAQ.

I was reminded of this when I recently appeared on the front page of *The Business Times* here in Singapore. The last time I was on the front page of a newspaper over here was five years ago, and it was due to a blog I wrote about Singaporean taxi drivers. That blog led me to being fired from my role at the time, and it was one of the most stressful times in my life.

Not only was I featured in the tabloid rag, *The New Paper,* but I was also featured in every other newspaper in Singapore, as well as every Chinese, Malaysian, Tamilian, and English paper. I was also featured on Channel News Asia and Asia One websites, not to mention a million other online chat rooms and discussion forums, and this is where I really got to know the underbelly of Singapore.

Trolling has nothing on anonymous Singaporean writers who are enraged by an expat who writes something they disagree with, and who use it as an excuse to abuse all expats for stealing their jobs/women/train seat/car lane/food centre seat/HDB/life/free gift from McDonald's/last Krispy Creme doughnut, etc. It was where I first started enjoying debates with anonymous trolls who don't consider facts and just want to unleash venom!

Locals in my office at the time ensured that my ultimate boss in the UK got to see the front page, out of context, of course, which resulted in my suspension. Two weeks later, I was fired. It was painful but warranted. Even though I had maintained a personal blog, everything you do on social media reflects on your profession and your company. Even though my blog piece was based on evidence, it didn't reflect well on the company I worked for at the time. I could have written it better, but you learn from your mistakes.

I still find it amazing now that people on LinkedIn don't comprehend that what they post on LinkedIn represents their company as well as themselves. Everyone can see who you work for, so technically, everything you post is being either positively or negatively associated with and endorsed by the company you work for. That's why I always recommend thinking twice before posting on LinkedIn, particularly if you're the boss like I am.

Are your boss and your boss's boss (who are often in a different country) going to approve it if they see it? Your personal brand is your professional brand, and unless, and even if, you remove all company associations, a quick search on Google will reveal who you work for.

The controversy actually didn't stop me getting taxis, despite the fact that *The New Paper* created a graphic that said in Chinese, 'Beware of this Man!'

The irony was that many expats mostly agreed with my blog, but unlike me, they had the good sense to leave it out of a blog, and those who did not agree with me still saw my point of view. Many locals also agreed with me; at least, they agreed face to face! Also, it didn't stop me getting future jobs or winning business.

The experience gave me brand recognition and even elicited sympathy from people, some of whom said that I was harshly treated by my former employer, by anonymous trolls online, and the media, even if they disagreed with what I did and said.

It became a talking point that enabled me to use it as a way to go from a negative to a positive at a business meeting, and it opened up a dialogue to discuss what I could do for that person in a professional capacity. They would then look beyond that controversy to consider what I could actually do for them.

Controversy is often essential to a personal brand, especially one like mine. I run a small SME and am trying to stand out against multinationals and other social media agencies who are trying to specialise in LinkedIn and supposed LinkedIn trainers, many of whom don't even use the platform themselves.

I live and breathe it. I regularly meet people from LinkedIn who know 5% of what I know about the platform; some of these people are great sellers, but they are not great LinkedIn users, and in my opinion, they're, therefore, not the best advocates of LinkedIn. Consequently, I demonstrate through everything from my blogs to my Mohawk how you can use personal branding to elevate your company, gain brand recognition and awareness, and drive your business, especially in countries/cities where no one knows you. People buy people in every walk of life.

I am from Newcastle upon Tyne in the true north of England, and where I come from people are very direct. They speak their minds and tell you the truth, directly and without care of consequence. 'Better to be true to yourself than fake', Geordies say. Marketing has a hard job in Newcastle! This is why I moved 500 kilometres south to London where they tend to believe things more readily and marketing works more easily.

My blogs follow this adage, as does my sales pitch. As my many clients would testify, I will tell you how terrible your LinkedIn profile, personal brand, social selling, and content marketing is before demonstrating what you should be doing and how you can use the platform to win clients and enhance your personal brand. Fellow entrepreneurs appreciate my honesty. I'm not smooth-talking them; instead, I'm giving it to them straight. Not everyone appreciates my style, but everyone at least knows I'm saying it from the heart, and even if they don't use us to enhance their LinkedIn marketing, they can see what they are missing out on, and they go and do it for themselves.

I wrote the notorious blog after success on another one about why Singaporeans need to look at experience above qualifications. *Singapore*

Business Review numbers were being propelled to record numbers by my blogs. The publisher, Tim, felt so thankful that it started a great friendship between us. I shared the blogs on LinkedIn, and people were driven to his website through it. Of course, controversy also drives numbers, and during the time of my taxi blog, his numbers went up 33% to 250,000 viewers.

Nevertheless, there is a fine line between ranting, like in my taxi blog, versus being skillfully provocative, like in my blog about valuing experience over qualifications. When people started a campaign to get me kicked out of the country, it was people like Tim and the Singaporean lawyer that Tim recommended who ensured that I wasn't. It was at the time of several other more infamous and notorious cases of expats, who were kicked out/hounded out of the country. I am the only survivor!

Of course, it made me look at things differently: I wouldn't recommend the experience to anyone, but it hardens you up and makes you more aware of your actions and responsibilities as a guest in someone else's country. I am a permanent resident in Singapore, and it is very much my home after eight years now. I hope to become a citizen one day, even if that means giving up my British passport.

To this day, my experience is something that people still discuss, and of course, there are still traces about it on Google. Fortunately, all my more noteworthy achievements in business since then take priority in my Google search results, but type, 'Chris Reed Taxi Singapore', and you still can find a hundred forums of hate from the time.

The irony is that the adage 'all publicity is good publicity' is actually true in this case although I didn't think so at the time! It gave me name recognition beyond my circle and beyond LinkedIn. To this day, people still refer to me as 'infamous' as a result of it.

Since then, I have built my personal brand and learned from my experience: I am still forthright because I believe that all blogs should be that way, but I think that society is more accepting of more provocative content, and there are just more blogs out there with far more outrageous things in them.

When I wrote this, there were fewer people writing blogs and fewer people on LinkedIn to share. You can see that in the numbers SBR blogs attract now. I got 50,000 views for both those blogs, but these days, any blog on SBR is lucky to reach 5,000. There is more competition, more choices, and more platforms.

The experience directly led me to create Black Marketing—Enabling LinkedIn for You. This happened both because of my terrible employment choices after I was fired, but also because the experience gave me a greater understanding of the culture, the people, and the region. With name recognition and the enhanced personal branding that my notoriety gave me, I was in a strong position to launch Black Marketing with confirmed clients. It was a running start.

Since then, we have gone from strength to strength, won awards, produced the #1 international best-selling book about LinkedIn, won LinkedIn Power Profile status six years running, floated on NASDAQ as the founding company of The Marketing Group Plc, and every year we beat the previous year for clients and revenue. I even appeared on Channel News Asia's *Coffee with the Boss.*

All of these milestones led to *The Business Times* featuring me on their front cover. They wrote about how I was the only marketing entrepreneur who placed LinkedIn as central to their business model out of all the Power Profiles featured. Not only was I servicing entrepreneurs for their LinkedIn marketing strategies, but I was actually using LinkedIn myself to enhance my personal brand, company brand, content marketing, and for lead generation. I was effectively proving it worked.

In 5 years, I went from being fired and having nothing to creating a successful NASDAQ-listed company. I went from being an outcast to: Even if I wasn't an ideal example of an expat in Singapore, I certainly had the business credentials to back up what I do and say. I also do much more from a non-profit, community, and goodwill point of view, because I embrace my responsibilities as an expat entrepreneur. Ninety percent of my 25 staff in Singapore is, in fact, Singaporean.

I mentor SMU Marketing graduates and have done so for 4 years now, I regularly speak at Singaporean organisations to graduates and young Singaporeans (for example, to NUS at NUSS above and NTUC, La Salle, and SICC), and I also speak at education establishments to spread the word about LinkedIn. In addition, I give back to the country and its people where I have created a successful LinkedIn marketing business, and I now very much call Singapore my home. I am also a board director and chair of the Marketing Business Group for the British Chamber of Commerce, where I evangelise about marketing best practice to both members and non-members.

Chapter Five

The Only CEO with a Mohawk—My Personal Branding

I love my Mohawk. These are four words I never envisaged uttering when I first came to sunny Singapore! Now I couldn't imagine going anywhere without it! Using the personal branding strap-line, 'The only CEO with a Mohawk!' on my LinkedIn also works; people smile and remind me about it when we first meet. This is personal branding using content and social media, and at zero cost. Anyone can do it. You can do it; it's a personal choice to use yourself to market your company. It's not for everyone, but it is fun!

Everywhere I go in Singapore, and in fact all over Asia Pacific, everyone either: 1) says, 'I love your hair', or 'Cool hair'; 2) recognises me because of my LinkedIn photo with my Mohawk, or 3) points at me and giggles/laughs/smiles (usually little kids pointing me out to daddy/mummy who then smile knowingly). Money can't buy this level of personal brand recognition.

My Mohawk is a real ice-breaker. I go through the strictest security to enter countries or buildings, and even the most hard-nosed security guards or passport control guards say, 'Love your hair', 'Cool hair', or just smile knowingly. It's a great feeling to make someone you have never met smile using something as simple a hairstyle for personal branding.

My Mohawk is a must-have at all the events where I attend and speak. I generate acres of social media coverage purely because people who attend take pictures of me performing with my Mohawk or because they wish to have their photo taken with me because of my Mohawk. It's a unique reason to share, it enhances my personal brand, and consequently, it enhances my company brand, Black Marketing—Enabling LinkedIn for You, which offers the service of personal branding. I believe you should live what you preach; don't be the tale of the cobbler's kids who have the worst shoes!

The colour of my Mohawk changes depending on my mood and what I fancy doing next to generate discussion or elicit a call to action. From purple to green to orange to LinkedIn blue (the new colour I named!) to pink to red. White could be next, but I would look like a skunk!

The reason I am using the personal branding strap-line, 'The only CEO with a Mohawk', is that I do appear to be the only CEO with a Mohawk, at least in my biggest markets, Singapore, Hong Kong, and Shanghai. Instant personal brand recognition is something that money cannot buy in these days of overloaded content, newsfeeds that are increasingly overlooked, emails, WhatsApp, Skype, WeChat, and all types of marketing messages.

Amongst my target audience of entrepreneurs, founders, CEOs, and marketing people, it's perfect. People respect it and love it. It's a real talking point, and people often then tell me stories about what they do/ have done that gives them individuality too, as well as what enhances their personal brand. They also tell me stories of when they were young and were a punk, but now that they are in corporate world, they believe they cannot. I, of course, ask, 'Why not?!' But, I know it's not for everyone. In fact, if it were, I wouldn't be 'the only CEO with a Mohawk!'

I can also see that I put myself out there to be shot down, but so be it. The upside in places like Singapore, Hong Kong, and Shanghai, is so much better than any downside. I make more people smile, think, and remember me than not; that's a great feeling as a marketing professional. It also obviously promotes my business, which in turn, helps create awareness and interest in our services, which is content marketing using my personal brand to market our LinkedIn marketing services.

As an entrepreneur of an SME in Singapore, my Mohawk is designed to create awareness of my personal brand and be noticed everywhere I go, which is especially relevant for business events that make you think about your personal brand. It is literally everywhere I go: from lifts in malls in Hong Kong, to gyms in Manilla; from restaurants in Singapore and walking down the street in Shanghai, to airport lounges in Jakarta, Sydney, Singapore, and Shanghai. Clearly, business lounges in airports are the place to go to meet people because that's where I have been recognised several times by people due to my Mohawk!

Everywhere I go, there is someone who has either seen me do a talk or someone who has seen me on LinkedIn. 'The only CEO with a Mohawk' works as a branding strap-line. This is an amazing call to action and enables people to come up to me and say, 'Hey, you're the only CEO with a Mohawk', or 'Hey, you're Mr. LinkedIn'. It's a great ice-breaker. We both smile.

It's what I call the Richard Branson effect. You know about Virgin, the Virgin brand, and the Virgin companies because of Richard Branson. You buy into Branson and his entrepreneurial ethos and personal brand because of his stunts, blogging, and social media presence. He has 9 million followers on LinkedIn, which is more than Apple, Google, and Facebook combined.

Who is the number one most viewed profile on LinkedIn? Candice Galek, CEO and founder of Bikini Luxe. She only has 40,000 followers, some 8.5 million less than Richard Branson and 4.5 million less than Bill Gates. Yet, she has the most viewed LinkedIn profile out of 440 million LinkedIn professionals. Why?

Amazing personal branding and incredibly focused, simple, and effective content marketing. Her business is bikinis, and she shares photos of her business. She writes blogs about all kinds of things and highlights her content with pictures of her business (bikinis). On a social media network that's dominated by males, her social media network works for her. On a professional network with fellow female entrepreneurs, her network works for her. Epic content marketing, brilliant personal branding: Hats off to Candice.

I recently read a brilliant book by James Watts, who is the cofounder of BrewDog. This founder boasts the most successful craft beer and fastest-growing food and beverage brand and restaurant in the UK, and his book is called Business for Punks. The book is all about how they used content, stunts, and social media to create a multimillion-dollar consumer brand and to make a profit every year since the company's inception.

BrewDog spent no money on media, creative agencies, or advertising; they just used what they had, and it worked fantastically well (ironically James Watt is not on LinkedIn, but his cofounder, Martin Dickie, is). Nevertheless, Martin is not using LinkedIn to maximum effect.

The same applies to you and your personal brand. You don't need money or advertising; you just need an angle or a reason for people to remember you. The rest is down to your personality, ability to communicate your business, and accentuate relationships. But it starts with your personal brand recognition, just as it does for any B2C or B2B brand. You are a brand, with brand values and attributes, just like any brand is.

When I google you, the first thing that comes up is your LinkedIn profile, just like it does with me. When I then click on that, I gain an impression and a general perception of you, based on what is on your profile. That's your brand: The perception of you that I have in my mind.

The content that you have added, your picture, your strap-line (if you have one), your keywords (if you're using them), your summary section, your background picture, your experience section, what else you do apart from your job, associations, awards, speaking engagements, books? Everything you put on your LinkedIn profile, or anything you miss on your LinkedIn profile, creates your personal brand in my mind or in the mind of anyone else who views your profile. That is your brand.

In his book, James Watt describes how BrewDog does not own the brand. The customers do. They make it what it is. A brand is what other people perceive it as. A brand is in the mind of a consumer, whether it's B2B or B2C. You are in charge of your personal brand and how that is perceived. What you do on LinkedIn creates that impression, because that is often the first place someone finds out about or experiences your personal brand.

You have to take responsibility for your brand; otherwise, other people will form an impression and create it for you. You're in charge. You are your own brand guardian.

In that context, it was a no-brainer to use the photo of my Mohawk on the front cover of my international best-selling book, *LinkedIn Mastery for Entrepreneurs*, even though it was against both my publisher's advice and conventional wisdom.

Apparently, you don't use a photo on your book unless the photo enhances its ability to sell, and most authors are not known visually. Mine very clearly stands out as a business book on both the virtual and 3D shelves. Since we offer the service of personal branding, there was no question that I had to use it, and more importantly, it worked.

My picture now appears on both my books. The blue matches my brand, Black Marketing—Enabling LinkedIn for You, while the red is my branding for The Dark Art of Marketing—Personal Branding for Entrepreneurs.

One of the amazing aspects of having a Mohawk is that it always generates a discussion with normally sane- minded and business-focused executives about how my Mohawk stays up. Bearing in mind that I live on a tropical island (Singapore) where average temperatures are currently at 34-36 degrees Celsius, with 60-90% humidity and daily torrential rain, gels and waxes don't work.

I use Gatsby Designer Clay, and this revelation is a real catalyst for a discussion about hair products, how long it takes to keep up, how often I have it done, whether I do it myself every day, or have a team of experts(!), etc. Metro-sexual men and those who appear to be least likely to ever happily discuss hair products actually do exactly that, along with many women who seem to be generally more at ease discussing hair products and personal presentation. It's another great ice-breaker, and everyone invariably goes away smiling.

The Mohawk is part of my personal brand while 'The only CEO with a Mohawk' is my personal branding strap-line. It stands out on the cover of my book, and it naturally accompanies a photo of my LinkedIn blue Mohawk. The picture and strap-line are totally appropriate for a book about LinkedIn for entrepreneurs that is founded on the premise that your personal brand is communicated through LinkedIn.

You are your personal brand. Your LinkedIn profile is what communicates that 24/7. Isn't NOW the time to take action with yours? Start with your very own version of my Mohawk and accentuate it from there.

Good luck, have fun doing it, and make someone smile!

Chapter Six

Be More American and Less English in Your Personal Branding

'I'm self-deprecating because I'm British. If I was American, I'd tell you how great I was'. This is not a quote from me; it's a quote from James Blunt. No, I'm not a fan, but I read a very amusing interview with him in *The Guardian* recently. He's very self-aware, and he's highly conscious of his personal brand, what people say about him, and of cultural nuances. Nevertheless, this quote is common amongst many of my non-American clients and in some of my clients in Asia Pacific.

I always tell my clients to be 'less English and more American': To be less modest and more assertive and confident about communicating what they have actually done and are capable of doing. Being more assertive and confident doesn't mean lying or exaggerating; it's just about saying how you led your team that won that award, that you broke new ground, you innovated that product, changed a loss to profit, and it specifies your actual role in each of your achievements.

If you don't do it, then there will always be an American who will quite happily do it instead. So, it's your loss and their gain. It's up to you. Compete on the same playing field, or lose out.

I love this quote because it really sums up how people don't read and understand music lyrics, and instead, take everything at face value. The lesson is that people should delve more deeply into meanings of words and really look at words in their context. It is just like on LinkedIn: Look at the detail, look at the depth, and look at the evidence to back up the claims. Don't just take everything at face value.

Just because someone says that they're an expert at something, it doesn't mean that they are unless they can back it up. An example of misinterpreting the written word is the song, 'Born in the USA'. Most people don't realise that the song is not about patriotism. Also, the Police's 'Every Breath You Take' is definitely not a love song, and in the context of this post, nor is James Blunt's most famous song 'You're Beautiful'. It's hugely touching that people play 'You're Beautiful' at their weddings. But, if you listen to the lyrics, it's about a guy who's high as a kite on drugs who is stalking someone else's girlfriend on the train. It's not romantic; it's twisted.

Chapter Seven

My ANZ Interview on My Personal Branding

Chris J. Reed has significantly grown his business by harnessing the social platform of LinkedIn and via teaching others how to do the same.

It's taken Chris Reed less than two years to grow his company, Black Marketing, from a one-man operation in Singapore to a NASDAQ-traded company operating in dozens of countries globally.

His success is due to an unusual business model: It relies on the LinkedIn social media platform, where his profile is one of the most viewed on LinkedIn worldwide, earning him a coveted 'Power Profile' status.

His success is in spite of, and perhaps because of, adopting a hairstyle that is unusual in the business world: He sports a colourful Mohawk. Reed contends that neither the edgy company name, Black Marketing, nor the Mohawk have alienated potential clients.

He admits that both his company name and personal image defy conformity, with Black Marketing a compelling and clever reference to the dark art of marketing. The company uses a three-person team to manage each client account, and their priorities are all about helping others to learn how to make a real splash on the LinkedIn platform.

'Our clients talk about us, we take over their LinkedIn profiles, and we tell people how to do LinkedIn, but most importantly, we implement LinkedIn strategies for CEOs, entrepreneurs, and people who are too busy to do it themselves', Reed explains.

'The company name hints at an underground movement; that's a deliberate strategy', he adds.

'It's the behind-the-scenes thing; we make people superstars on LinkedIn, and hence the black marketing', says Reed.

Put simply, they specialise in making people stand out on LinkedIn, and Reed stands out with his various coloured Mohawks. It's been blue in the past, but it is currently red.

'At a party in Singapore, I was approached by a guy who said, 'You're the guy on LinkedIn'. He didn't know me, but saw the blue Mohawk and associated it with my LinkedIn branding', says Reed.

Despite the rebellious image, many of Black Marketing's clients are traditionally conservative.

Originally from the UK, Reed completed a marketing degree and worked in marketing for nearly two decades within publishing and hospitality companies before he moved to Singapore eight years ago.

The move to Singapore sparked Reed's interest in LinkedIn, which he saw as a useful networking tool. Reed landed his first marketing contract via a LinkedIn connection, and at that point, his profile rapidly gained influence.

Others started to approach him for advice on managing their LinkedIn profile, which led Reed to recognise a potential business opportunity.

'Smart people will think about pitching their service to potential clients that are already out there. I was already winning LinkedIn Power Profile awards when I was working for other companies. If you do some research, you can judge pretty well whether it is going to work', said Reed.

The increasing demand was so strong that Reed says when he launched Black Marketing, he skipped the traditional start-up phase, and within two years of launching, floated his fast-growing company on the NASDAQ exchange.

Reed says that he developed the plans for his new business outside office hours whilst he was still an employee—a strategy he recommends, noting that it's important to have an income when preparing to work for yourself.

By the end of his first year in business (2014), Black Marketing's daily operations were solely financed by clients. Reed then sold his house in the UK to help fund the growth of his company as he began employing people and expanding internationally.

Reed says that having a proven strategy for LinkedIn (demonstrated through his own profile) has secured him a diverse client base, with 90% of the SME space.

'SMEs are the best people to do LinkedIn as they know they need to use their personal brand to win business, clients, employees, and investors', he says.

'People buy into Black Marketing because of me, and I must elevate my personal brand to maintain our LinkedIn presence. Multinationals can afford to wait for business to come to them, but SMEs do not have that luxury', said Reed.

'Believe in yourself and promote yourself, your awards, and your achievements'.

Being Singapore-based has given Reed insight into the cultural differences in personal branding in Asia.

'Like the English, Asian entrepreneurs don't like promoting themselves, but US entrepreneurs find it quite straightforward', he says.

Reed says that when he talks to Asian and British clients, he points out ways to ensure that personal branding is highlighting their professional achievements and skills. He cites Richard Branson, who is a natural introvert, as an example of using personal branding to compete against established competitors.

Reed has drawn another benefit from his company's unusual branding: Black Marketing has become an attractive employment option for millennials because Reed doesn't impose a conservative dress code and clearly has a high tolerance for hair dyes, tattoos, and piercings.

And finally, Reed says that the LinkedIn platform can offer SMEs a level playing field where, with time and effort, SME founders can obtain the same traction as global multinationals.

Chapter Eight

My Channel News Asia Interview on My Personal Branding

Coffee with the Boss Host: Chris J. Reed sure knows how to turn heads when he walks into a room. Chris J. Reed is the only NASDAQ chief executive with a Mohawk. Let's sit down with the global CEO and founder of Black Marketing. On *Coffee with the Boss,* we sit down with founder and CEO of Black Marketing, Chris J. Reed. Chris has taken his company from one person in one country in 2014 to a full listing on NASDAQ in 2016.

He was awarded Asia's Most Influential Digital Media Professional by CMO, Asia. This man has one of the most viewed LinkedIn profiles, with 55,000 followers, and for six years now, he has had a LinkedIn Power Profile. His late grandfather always told him that it's not what you know; it's who you know. Could he be dead right?

Interviewing Journalist: Chris, you're a marketing guru, so I want to pick your brain: With the economy slowing down, how do you stay ahead in terms of branding and marketability?

Chris: Excellent question. It's all about your personal brand; your personal brand is what takes your business forward. You are the leader of your company, you are the leader of your team, and you are in charge of your own personal brand and your destiny. So, you have to invest in your personal brand.

Interviewing Journalist: When it comes to personal branding, you talk about the executive branding of someone. Can you explain in more detail what exactly that means?

Chris: If I google you, for example, the first thing that comes up is your LinkedIn profile. So I look at it, and I get an impression of you, which is either positive or negative. What does it include? What does it include and what does it not include? Does it talk about your business? Does it talk about your awards and achievements, and your associations?

If you fill it with thought leadership and content marketing, talk about your career and what you have done, then you will create a positive impression. If you don't do any of these things, people will have a negative impression of you and move on to someone else. So, it's up to you: You can fill it with fantastic content. Alternatively, you can choose not to and lose out.

Interviewing Journalist: Do Asians make use of executive branding, or are they a bit too shy?

Chris: No; they're absolutely terrible. I call it the less-English-and-less-Asian-and-the-more-American way to market yourself, but not so American that you think that you've invented the entire world, but more in terms of the fact that you have actually put your achievements out here. English people are similar to Asian people: They're very modest and don't want to talk about their achievements, or don't want to be seen as promoting themselves.

But, you have to because there will be an American or an Australian out there doing it for you, so you have to overcome the fact that it's your personal brand and go into your business brand. It's business on LinkedIn; it's not personal. It's about you as a business brand.

Interviewing Journalist: So what exactly should people be doing? Should they be accentuating the positives of what they have?

Chris: Very much so, and talking about their careers. So for example, I could talk about going to Singapore without a job, talk about how I used LinkedIn to get my first job, talk about how I used LinkedIn to get on NASDAQ, the awards I have won, and talk about how I became an official marketing partner of the British Chamber and the American Chamber of Commerce.

All of these things are talking points that add to my personal brand. They are my brand values: Just like Nike, Apple, and Coca-Cola have brand views, so do you, and so does everyone else. You have to put the information in there because people don't know about it unless you tell them about it. You cannot expect people to think, 'That's amazing', if you don't say what you have done.

Interviewing Journalist: You are the only CEO with a Mohawk who has a NASDAQ listing.

Chris: Indeed, very much so, and that's my personal brand. I was in Shanghai last week at a museum, and somebody came up to me and said, 'You don't know me, but we're connected on LinkedIn; you're Mr. NASDAQ. You're Mr. Mohawk; you're Mr LinkedIn'.

I was in Hong Kong a week before in a mall. Somebody said, 'Wow. I remember you did a talk two years ago for LinkedIn. I recognise the Mohawk'. It's so distinctive, especially somewhere like Singapore, Hong Kong, or Shanghai, which are very conservative societies. You stand out by putting yourself out there; you will get noticed. Then, you have to back it up with substantial things to make sure that you follow through. You've got to match the two together. It's all about a point of difference: An icebreaker too.

Interviewing Journalist: What are people doing wrong when it comes to marketing in the 21st century?

Chris: They're underestimating what they should do. So, they're using things like Facebook and WeChat, which might have a billion or two billion users, but they're the wrong kind of users if you want a professional network. You have to think about it in a professional context; who do you want to be seen by? Who do you want to target in a professional network?

That's why I love LinkedIn so much: It's about you and your company. You know where people come from, you know what that company is, you know where their standing comes from. The problem with Facebook and Twitter is that not all countries use these platforms. WeChat is popular in China but not the rest of Southeast Asia, for example. LinkedIn is the only business network that's truly global. So, people have to think about the context of what they share. So, something on Facebook is not right for LinkedIn; something on LinkedIn is not right for Facebook.

So, you have to think about how you share; don't just share something for the sake of it. Share, whilst keeping in mind what impact you want the content to have on someone from a professional point of view and also what impact you want to have from a friends-and-family point of view. It's very different.

Interviewing Journalist: Is it the sort of thing that you picked up from your grandfather because I believe he said, 'It's not what you know, it's who you know'?

Chris: Definitely; at nine years old, I was saying, 'What you mean? Surely, I will just go to university and get a degree and get a job, and that's it', but no. As I went through my career, I realised that it's all about networking. My clients from my first, my second, my third, my fourth, and my fifth jobs all became my clients when I launched my company in my thirties.

I stayed in touch with these networks and then connected to them later. When LinkedIn came along, it was even more amazing, especially in Asia, where everyone is so positive. What I love about Asia is that I reached out here, and people said yes. People in the UK would not say yes. In the UK, it was like: 'No, in 6 months time, or in 9 months time', if you're lucky. Whereas here, they say, 'Let's have coffee tomorrow'.

People embrace it here, both the expats and the locals. It's so positive in Asia, not just Singapore, but Southeast Asia, Hong Kong, and Shanghai have such a positive environment. People want to meet you: Across all cultures and all creeds. It's absolutely fantastic.

Interviewing Journalist: You have a real vibrancy about you. You must be quite a boss at work.

Chris: {Laughs} I am sure my staff wouldn't necessarily say that. I am very demanding. I get up at 5 o'clock in the morning. I cycle to work and I energise myself and I love it. I work 15 or 16 hours per day, every day of the week. I am in Shanghai, Hong Kong, and Sydney all the time, and I spend a lot of time in Singapore and countries in Southeast Asia. I am in different countries talking about LinkedIn, and I am very passionate about it.

I also expect my staff to be passionate and to know every single thing. If I see you on your phone, I get annoyed straightaway. Not all of them can take it, and not all of them can follow it, but the really fantastic ones do: They aspire to it, they grow with it, and they take that challenge, but it's not for everybody.

Interviewing Journalist: Tell me: What are the most important values to you?

Chris: Very much the values of authenticity, integrity, enthusiasm, and being driven. Being enthusiastic, driven, and passionate about your work is so important; I think that supersedes everything in life. I love entrepreneurs who are so passionate about their work. It doesn't matter whether they've got one customer or 1,000 customers, they're passionate about the impact they have on that particular customer, and I love seeing the effect that we have on our customers using LinkedIn; it's amazing.

Interviewing Journalist: Can I ask how many coffees you've had?

Chris: {Laughs}

Coffee with the Boss Host: Chris J. Reed, full of beans, full of coffee beans.

Chapter Nine
Personal Branding Tips on LinkedIn and Beyond

Mojo Radio Show Interview

Radio Host: I met this guy through LinkedIn, and he approached me to invite me to a gig whilst he was in Australia. The more I read and saw what he was doing, the more I knew we had to have him on the show. Something he spoke with me about is that everyone is on LinkedIn, but like me and most people, we don't know how to use it.

I always wanted to find someone who is an expert on LinkedIn to show me how to use it. Everybody connects with you and everyone is doing stuff, but it just overwhelms me, and I never know if what I am doing actually works. So, I invited Chris J. Reed, who is an international, award-winning author and an award-winning speaker, his agency is on NASDAQ, and it is an agency that specialises in LinkedIn.

He is pretty much the man on LinkedIn and everything to do with LinkedIn. We have him on the line right now. Chris J. Reed, welcome to the Mojo Radio Show.

Chris: Great to be here with you.

Radio Host: Now, you're Singapore-based, but we have found you here, on tour, in Australia. What's your tour all about Down Under?

Chris: Well, the talk is about LinkedIn. It's about how to use LinkedIn, what it is used for, how to become a thought leader, how to generate business, how you use it for employer branding, how to enhance your personal brand, and how you can use LinkedIn to target the nine million people on LinkedIn in Australia.

Radio Host: So, if people ask you what you do on a day-to-day basis, what do you say? Who would you be doing it with and for?

Chris: I personally evangelise about LinkedIn on a non-stop basis. I have done talks today, I have had meetings today, and then I train my team when I am in Singapore to deliver what we're selling. So, basically, we're selling like 10 services.

Essentially, we are a LinkedIn service that enhances your personal brand: We create a company brand, we create a content marketing strategy, and we create a thought leadership strategy. If you were a CEO, founder, or entrepreneur, we create a social selling tool that generates you new leads on LinkedIn. So, I trained my team how to do that. We do that for our clients, and I go out there and sell it to entrepreneurs, SMEs, founders, CEOs, and whoever needs it, and whoever I think needs it.

Radio Host: So why is your interest in LinkedIn? You have been awarded, you have written about it, you've built an agency in Singapore around it, and you're now on the speaking circuit. Why the interest in LinkedIn for you personally?

Chris: I came to Asia 8 years ago, and I didn't know a single person, so I had to reach out using people I knew on LinkedIn in the UK. I said to these people: 'Who do you know in Singapore? Connect me with somebody in Singapore'. Then I started connecting with people in Singapore, and people started saying, 'Yes, I'll meet you, Chris. Yes, I'll have a coffee with you'.

They had no reason to do so, but because I reached out to them on LinkedIn, they said yes. When I got my first job, it was through LinkedIn. It wasn't an advertised job. I got my second job on LinkedIn, and again, it wasn't advertised, and both these jobs were regional work: A regional development role and a regional marketing role. I had no contacts in Asia Pacific, but I started using LinkedIn to reach out to people, and people started saying yes, and not just in

Singapore, but in Australia and Japan and Indonesia and China and India, and right across the whole country and the whole region.

So it's really exciting to actually break into these kinds of markets using the power of LinkedIn. Then, people started asking me to train them and to train their sales team, their marketing team, and their C-suite, using LinkedIn. Then, people started asking me to actually do their profiles on LinkedIn because I started winning awards from LinkedIn itself.

So, I knew there was a business there. As soon as 2014 hit, I basically created Black Marketing. I knew there were many clients waiting for me to basically hit them, start working with them, enhance their personal brand on LinkedIn, and create a content marketing plan on LinkedIn. So, there was a ready-made audience there for me. We started pushing it out and marketing it across the region.

It became bigger and bigger and bigger, and that's why we floated on NASDAQ last year because we became so big: We had clients across the world, not just here in Australia, but across Asia Pacific, across Southeast Asia and Singapore, Hong Kong, and Shanghai, and Europe, including London, Paris, Amsterdam, and then places like New York and California.

So it's a global phenomenon that nobody else is really doing. There's a real niche in the market. Nobody else is doing exactly what we're doing.

Radio Host: You said you contacted people. You said it's going back a few years. You arrived in Singapore, and you didn't know anyone. If I establish a LinkedIn profile, how do I go about talking to somebody or making contact with somebody?

Chris: What's interesting for me is that lead generation for anybody seems to be one of the biggest issues in business. People come in, they hit the low-hanging fruit, but when it comes down to making contacts, getting business, and opening doors, there seems to be a problem for people.

Radio Host: You've said that was one of the primary advantages of using LinkedIn. How specifically? What are the steps to doing that?

Chris: Well, first of all you have to create a personal brand: If you have no personal brand on LinkedIn, you will fail to deliver leads because if you don't have a photograph, you don't have a strap-line, you don't have any connections, you don't have a summary section, you don't have a company page, then nobody will take you seriously. So, you have to create all of this first; you have to create a personal brand. Then, you have to make sure you have a company brand on LinkedIn.

If you're an SME or you're an entrepreneur, you cannot overlook the fact that you need a company brand on LinkedIn. If you don't have a company page on LinkedIn, no one will take you seriously. They will think you're just a sole trader. Then, you need a content marketing strategy. You then need a thought leadership strategy.

If you are one of the 10% to actually bother doing this on LinkedIn, you will raise yourself above everyone else on LinkedIn. People will take you seriously, but more importantly, you will drive people to your profile. You will drive people to actually want to know more about you from a personal brand point of view. If they approach you on LinkedIn due to the content marketing that you shared or you created, you can then approach them and say, 'Thank you very much for liking, sharing, commenting on my content, and viewing my profile'.

I will say, 'I want to talk to you about my service', and they will say yes because they've already approached you. You have used content to instigate and to inspire them to come to you. The other way of doing it is to basically build up your first connections, creating a relationship with them over time. Share content, participate, and engage with them on a daily basis, and then when you reach them for new business, they will say yes. The third way of doing it is the Sales Navigator platform, which is just a transforming platform about how to use all the data on LinkedIn.

There are 550 million professionals on LinkedIn, and I can find anybody, anywhere in the world in any company, and I can find clients for them. I can find them in America, in Europe, in Asia, in Australia, in Shanghai, and in Hong Kong. Wherever you want to find a client, I can find them on LinkedIn using the Sales Navigator platform. I can write them a personalised message for either myself or my clients, and actually make sure they return, they're interested, and they will potentially become a client.

Either I follow up with the lead if it's Black Marketing, or I pass it on to one of my clients if I am doing it for their profile. It's all about them, their profile, and their personal plans when we do this on LinkedIn.

Radio Host: Sales Navigator platform: Where do I find that? How do I use that? Can anybody access it? Is it a premium account service?

Chris: It's a premium account service, but it's about 60 or 70 bucks Australian for one version, and about 120 bucks for another version. You really need it to see the data because you can't see the profiles on LinkedIn unless you're premium, but not more importantly, it allows you to create target lists. It also allows you to actually see who's actually active on LinkedIn. Because, don't forget, 550 million people are on LinkedIn, but only about 120 million people are actually active on a monthly basis. Therefore, you're kind of wasting your time if you're targeting somebody who's not even active on LinkedIn.

So, we specialise in finding people who are actually active on LinkedIn, who are more likely to respond: they might have lots of shared connections with you or share common interests or universities. You personalise it to make sure that they actually say yes; I will respond to Darren because Darren has this many connections that I know, or Darren works in this company and I know people in that company, or Darren went to this university. So, you personalise it, and then you get a reaction. You get someone to say yes.

Radio Host: So, I think what we're saying here is that once I've got my profile up, and it's polished and sparkling, and I've got my premium account, I need to get to work with some due diligence. I need to do some research into the people that I might want to get in contact with, find out what they're doing on LinkedIn and the way they're doing it. I need to become a part of those conversations and start working from there. Does that sound right?

Chris: It's like real life. The more you take part in relationships in real life, the more you get out of it. If you don't participate and engage with your friends and your colleagues, you can't really expect them to come back to you. If you engage on LinkedIn on a professional basis with people who potentially become clients or peers, or just help you reach somebody else, they will respect you. You will help them, and they will help you, just like normal networking and normal professional relationships in the business world. LinkedIn just happens to be a virtual version of it.

Radio Host: Should I accept every invitation for someone to connect with me?

Chris: Yes, except if they are a general in Syria or they are an African dictator or they are an African dictator's wife or they are an African banker and they want your mother's maiden name, or they are a hooker in Estonia with a very dodgy summary section and seven connections. So, yes, apart from those people, of course! Why wouldn't you?

Radio Host: Chris, I've heard you talk about social selling. What's that?

Chris: Social selling is basically using social media to sell. And it's using content primarily to sell. You can't just expect to go on LinkedIn or go on any other platform and just basically sell straightaway. You have to create a brand, create engagement, give some content to people, share some interesting things, and participate in conversations, just like we would do in normal networking events. So, it's a social media sale using content to sell, and it's a soft sell.

We invite people to come to us, visit our profile, and come to me because I share relevant content about partnerships or about LinkedIn or about Australia or about a comment or about something that's interesting to them in their business. They then say, 'Oh, Chris must know what he is talking about'. They come to me and then they start a conversation about LinkedIn. It's a soft sell. It's never a hard sell. It's always, 'We could do this for you. We think we can achieve great things for you'. And you come to us because we share content or you know somebody I know or we work in the same company or we have just basically been recommended by somebody.

Radio Host: So if I break it down, I get a guy who is involved in his own small business or a lady who's running her own business from home selling through a website, what I'm hearing you say is that you've been successful through your business because people have come in and your personal brand or the business brand has been built on being a LinkedIn expert. If I go through that, you've got books, you've got awards, you immerse yourself in it. You've built your brand around that. Are you saying that people then need to make sure they have a distinct speciality that they're a thought leader in and a distinct point of difference that elevates them from their competition, so people will want to seek them out?

Chris: Of course! Like anything in life, you have to distinguish yourself, just like you distinguish yourself with your radio show. Everyone has to distinguish themselves. I distinguish myself by being a LinkedIn expert, by having a blue Mohawk or a red Mohawk, and by wearing black t-shirts when everyone else wears a suit.

I distinguish myself in lots of different ways by being unconventional, by being slightly more lateral in my thinking, but also in terms of saying, 'This is me. Accept me for who I am'. This is actually helping me build a business. I get recognised in Shanghai. I get recognised in Sydney.

I get recognised just by having a Mohawk because nobody else on LinkedIn has a Mohawk. So, if you have a Mohawk, whether it's a blue, green, red, or blonde Mohawk, you get noticed. But, I'm also a LinkedIn expert, so people come up to me and say, 'Oh, you're the Mohawk Guy. You're the LinkedIn guy'.

And they recognise me even though they've never met me before—just from the power of LinkedIn. Every single person on LinkedIn has to do the same thing. Everyone's got something unique to say. Everyone's got something unique about them and about what they do.

The biggest problem in Asia and in England and often in Australia as well is that people are too shy and people are too modest, and the problem with being too modest on LinkedIn is that there will be some American who will come along and claim your territory. There will be some American who comes along and says that they created the table or they created the air, even if it's not true.

Because they're American, people tend to believe them. You know, the whole Trump effect is achieved via hype over substance. But English people, Asians, and Australians actually did things first, but they don't like to say it because they're too modest. So, it's about bringing that out in a professional way. It's not boasting; it's not lying. It's not hyping yourself up.

It's just the truth. A lot of Asians are too modest, and a lot of Australians are too modest.

Radio Host: Can you give me an example of someone you've worked with that had a modest profile, but once they started working with you and your team, created an outstanding profile and a great personal brand that worked and actually attracted business through LinkedIn? Do you have an actual case study you could run us through?

Chris: Actually, I am obviously not allowed to tell you who we work for because you're not supposed to believe that the person you're interacting with online is not that person. You're supposed to believe you're talking to Richard Branson or Barrack Obama or Prime Minister Modi. You and I both know it's not those people involved, but you're supposed to believe it when you write, 'Yes, Richard.

That was a great blog', and you are supposed to believe that Richard Branson is writing back, 'Yes. I appreciate your input. Thank you very much for sharing'.

We know that it is not truly Richard Branson who is doing it, but that's the whole point. We take over the profiles of CEOs and founders. Well, I couldn't tell you who I was actually writing for, not least because I have these confidentiality agreements, but also because why would anyone trust me going forward if I told you who we worked for?

Radio Host: Pick a smaller, lesser-known person. I am not going to let you off the hook that easy. Chris, give me a smaller person and don't mention any names, but give me an example of 'Bob' or 'Mary'.

For instance, they owned a pet food company and this is what we did. This is how it changes. Give me one thing about someone in Hong Kong.

Chris: OK. We had an entrepreneur in Hong Kong. We took over his profile. He had like 100 connections. He didn't have any content marketing, and he was not connected to a company page. He was very successful, but he wanted to transform himself into a thought leader. So, we transformed his page, increased his connections to five thousand, and started winning lots and lots of contracts for him, and literally last week he told us he just won a million-dollar contract as a result of somebody responding to an email that we had sent on his behalf.

And he was so delighted with us that he recommended that we start work for the UK team. Now we work for the UK team, the Singapore team, and the Hong Kong team because success breeds success. He would not have got that million-dollar contract had we not beefed up his profile to build relationships and share content. We've got lots of case studies like that.

We have got people in Australia we worked for who were getting head-hunted, and for obvious reasons, I can't tell you who they are, but basically, we're beefing up their profile, so they leave the multinationals. The objective is to beef up their profile and to make sure that they basically become thought leaders so that someone goes, 'Wow. That's amazing. I just want that person in my organisation'.

We have an entrepreneur in Sydney: We've already won for him like three new clients since we starting working for him two months ago. We achieved this by beefing up his profile, adding key words, changing his picture, changing his summary section, adding a company page, adding some visuals, doing some video content, and making sure that he gets noticed.

Suddenly by just being noticed, people go, 'Wow. You are amazing. You are a thought leader in the digital marketing field. You've got to come in and pitch for us', and he paid me to pitch to this particular organisation in Australia, and he won. He wouldn't have got that invitation had he not got a beefed-up, search-orientated LinkedIn profile.

Radio Host: So, when people say, 'Chris J. Reed has endorsed you for . . . ' do those endorsements really carry weight?

Chris: That's a great question. Well, I use it in my presentations about what to do and then what not to do on LinkedIn. Don't get endorsed for PowerPoint, Excel, Word, and Office because people kind of assume you know how to use these things.

It is a bit like being endorsed for Google search or being able to use a smartphone. So, the trouble is that LinkedIn will do this if you don't tell them what you want to be endorsed for. So, you either play their game or you don't. So, you put the things you want to be endorsed for. For instance, I am endorsed for being a LinkedIn entrepreneur and for being a social media expert. But, if you don't do it, LinkedIn will suggest things to people, and they will endorse them just because of the gamification platform of LinkedIn.

So, we had a client the other day who was being endorsed for awesomeness and for general awesomeness, and he had no idea that people were endorsing him for being an awesome kind of guy. He thought, 'What the hell does that have to do with my business?'

Nothing at all. He was a financial adviser, but somehow LinkedIn had created awesomeness as being an endorsable skill, and because he had not changed his skills, people were endorsing him for being awesome.

Radio Host: What's the secret with groups? Do I just join groups that I feel reflect what I do? Do I need to join conversations? Do I just need to be a member of it for it to work for me? How do I work with groups?

Chris: The secret is not to join the group called the Daniel Robertson Appreciation Society; that's got two members, one of whom is your mum. There is basically no one in that group. Don't join the groups that sound funky and interesting. Join groups where your clients are and your peers are, and where your influencers are. These are normally 10, 20, 30, 40, 50 thousand, if not up to a million people. And the key there is to join by sharing content. When someone likes and when someone comments, you join the conversation. The worst thing you can do is share content, someone reacts, but you do not participate in a conversation with them.

It's all about having a conversation. It's all about sharing quality content, interesting content, and original content, and then participating in some kind of debate with them on LinkedIn in the groups, and other people will come in and actually debate with you as well. Then, they will start viewing your profile. If you have your key words right, they will then start finding out what you do. When they're interested in what you do because they've got to know you through the conversation, then that is typical social selling.

It's not about blasting stuff and spamming stuff about your company into the groups because it doesn't work at all. It's about sharing genuine information about things like the economy in Australia or about marketing or innovation in Australia, within an Australian innovation group on LinkedIn.

It's not about saying you have a great company and that you do innovation. It's about using content in a sophisticated way where you have a conversation with somebody in the same way you would at a networking event, and then you get to know them and they get to know you.

Then, you have a conversation offline. It is really about taking things offline. I have met dozens of entrepreneurs this week who are fantastic entrepreneurs, and I have really got to know them. But every single one of these conversations started on LinkedIn, and then I took them offline because you have the credibility online.

You take it offline and get to know someone better. Some of them become clients, some of them become partners, some of them become clients of the future, and some of them become advocates.

When they're interested in what you do because they've got to know you through the conversation, then that is typical social selling. It's not about blasting stuff and spamming stuff about your company in the groups because it doesn't work at all.

It's about sharing genuine information about things like the economy in Australia or about marketing or innovation in Australia, within an Australian innovation group on LinkedIn. It's not about saying you have a great company and that you do innovation.

Radio Host: Do you have to have a connection to have that conversation on LinkedIn?

Chris: No! In fact, it's better if you don't. Some of the best conversations we have are with second and third connections. If I have a connection with you, and I share something, and you connect with it, you share it, and you comment on it, it goes to all your connections. They then start a conversation, and I can then have a conversation with them as a result: I can see who likes it; I can see who shared it.

Then, the conversation spreads, and that's the beauty of LinkedIn. It is all about the three degrees of separation. If you have enough connections and you share content, it's engaging, and people start recognising you. I have got a couple of blogs going on LinkedIn at the moment.

I have lots of second and third connections whom I've never met before who are participating in a discussion that I have created. It's a really interesting discussion about business and about LinkedIn. It has taken on a life of its own because other people are taking it into their connections and their world. And they're seeing it as very useful content.

And that's the key to LinkedIn. It has to be useful and compelling content. There is lots of competition out there, so you have to make your content useful and compelling. It is not just about selling your services.

Radio Host: So, you have become an expert in LinkedIn, you're awarded, you've got books on it.

You have built a business on it. So, LinkedIn is your thing. I sit on a bus going into town, into any city on the way to work in the morning, or on a train, and I see people opening Facebook. Then they close that. Then they go into Twitter. They then close that.

Then they check Instagram, and then they check Facebook again. They might go into LinkedIn. So, they're going through all these platforms. In your mind, with the work you are doing, if you are a business person, are you better off just focusing on one platform, or in your mind, should they be across all platforms?

Chris: It's an excellent question because it depends on your industry. I can't say that LinkedIn is right for every single industry because it's clearly not. If you are a B2C industry, then LinkedIn is clearly wrong. But from a B2B point of view, you can attract employees and investors and PR, but you can't attract customers unless you are targeting high net worth individuals. So, if you're a B2B and most companies out there would be in some kind of way, then LinkedIn really is the only platform because you could be wasting a huge amount of time on Facebook and Twitter and Instagram.

If you are a B2B company and you are showing photographs of people who are basically students or people who are in their twenties and have no money, or basically people who are not business owners, then you are wasting your time. The thing about LinkedIn is that you know that everybody on there is professional. They're business owners, or they work for a business, and, therefore, your target audience is much more sophisticated, and you can tell exactly who they are.

On Facebook, how many people are fake, and how many people are bots in India? How many people are not real people? They're just basically there to bolster the numbers.

There are so many fake accounts on Facebook that you'd be so much more anonymous on Facebook and Twitter. Nobody uses Twitter. I live in Southeast Asia, and nobody uses Twitter in China. So, you're basically completely screwed if you're relying on one platform like that; whereas a platform like LinkedIn is in China, Indonesia, Japan, India, and it's right across the rest of world. It's the only professional network.

But again, it depends on who you are targeting. I am targeting entrepreneurs. I find them quite easily on LinkedIn across the world. However, if I were targeting millennials or teenagers in Australia, I would obviously use Facebook, Instagram, and Twitter, and I wouldn't be using LinkedIn, but if I were targeting nightclub owners who were targeting millennials, I would use LinkedIn because I'm not going to get them in enough numbers on things like Instagram or on Facebook. I can't tell where they are and who they are, but on LinkedIn, I can.

I can use the data to specify the owners of 25 nightclubs in Sydney and market to them directly. That's the beauty of LinkedIn; it's the data you input that everybody else can access. Nobody inputs the data on Instagram or Facebook that says someone is a nightclub owner in Sydney.

Radio Host: We've talked about content or data. What's your view of writing skills? You mentioned that Richard Branson does not do his own writing. You have talked about different people who might be outsourcing that.

The reason that I am interested in this is that I spoke to a girl recently, and she has changed jobs within a business. It is totally B2B. And the CEO has basically put her from a home-base, working on a laptop to write blogs. She said she is finding it really hard to create the tone of the CEO when you are not the CEO.

What it made me think about is that the skill of writing today seems to be very paramount in what we do. Whereas it used to be about doing PowerPoint slides, it's now about truly networking and not just going in and doing a presentation of my business to your business, but it is also now about creating content that intrigues you enough to spend time (a valuable asset) in reading and then engaging with me.

Run me through your view of today in regards to writing and creating content. Where's it at? What's great? What are we missing, what should we be doing?

Chris: Simply put, it has to be authentic. It needs to be original and compelling. So, the example you gave is a really good example. We come across that all the time where people say you can't possibly get to know me and write in my style. And yet we do so for hundreds of CEOs across the world because we spend the time to get to know them. And that's the key. If she's working remotely, then she can't really get to know him in an intimate way. Does he want to be controversial, does he want to be thought-provoking, does he want to be straightforward, and does he want to be funny?

What does he want to blog about? Then, we actually write in such a way that somebody else believes it is him. So you believe that Richard Branson's blogs are his, you believe that the Prime Minister's blogs are his, you believe that Barack Obama's blogs are his, and that all his responses are his as well. So, it's about creating compelling content and sharing compelling content that's actually interesting and authentic; it's something personal that you need to be briefed by.

A good example is that the CEO might brief this lady and say, 'I want to talk about my childhood and that I became an entrepreneur when my granddad said to me that it's not what you know, it's who you know, and this has basically set me on a course to identify LinkedIn as the key thing to do, and relationships and networking is the key to how I'm going to build a business'. I am actually going to tell that story because it's authentic, it's personal, but it's business at the same time, and someone can actually believe it.

So, it's about taking authentic things from the CEO and actually translating into something that's worthwhile reading on LinkedIn. Don't forget that LinkedIn is not Shakespeare, and it doesn't have to be Shakespeare. People overanalyse blogs and overcomplicate it. You know, you read it for a couple of minutes and then move on to the next one, and then if the headline does not catch you on the next one, you skip it. It's very hard to capture attention these days because, as you pointed out, people are not just competing on LinkedIn, they are competing on Instagram and Facebook and YouTube.

So, you've got to create something compelling and interesting. Therefore, I will share something that is interesting to me because this is interesting to others and it makes a difference. I will comment on it, I will like it, and I will share it. And that's the key. It's very hard to do. We will have an editorial team who do this and who are experts in doing this, but we don't get it right all the time. Nobody gets it right all the time.

Richard Branson's team doesn't get it right all the time. He doesn't get a million views for every single blog, and sometimes his blogs are terrible. Some of his blogs are fantastic, but he keeps on churning them out because he hopes there'll be one or two snippets in every single blog that make a difference to somebody and that make someone say, 'Richard Branson knows what I'm feeling. Richard Branson knows how to be an entrepreneur. I did learn something from Richard Branson that makes me a better entrepreneur'. And that's the gamble.

It's all about authentic content in a business context.

Radio Host: What's the thing that people don't know about LinkedIn? What don't we know?

Chris: Everything! That is why I am doing six talks this week in Sydney. Because despite the fact the city has 9 million people, and Australia has 9 million people on LinkedIn, nobody has a clue how to use LinkedIn. I'm not joking, either.

I've literally done a workshop this morning, and I am doing workshops this afternoon and workshops tomorrow morning, talking about how to use LinkedIn. I literally talk about how you block, how you share, how you use key words, how you use a background picture, and how you put up a profile picture. The people can actually see how you have a company page. You know, so it's not rocket science, but it's just basically pointing it out, and unfortunately LinkedIn themselves do not really help the situation because it's not very good at marketing. They are salespeople. They're salespeople in Singapore and Hong Kong. The creative guys and the operational guys are in San Francisco, and they don't really care about Asia.

Asia has 10 million people, and the US has 400 million people, but Asia is the fastest-growing region. So, I am teaching people about how to use LinkedIn, including just the basics about how to re-engage, how to block, how to share, and how to use key words so that you get found by people who want to find you.

So, it's basically everything. Sales Navigator is a classic one because nobody knows how to use Sales Navigator because no one knows Sales Navigator exists. And LinkedIn have not helped themselves at all by having three separate platforms, namely, Recruiter, Premium, and Sales Navigator. So, it's very hard to find Sales Navigator from the main LinkedIn platform. So, we basically do that for people, and we show people how to use it.

People's eyes just pop out of their heads when they see Sales Navigator and what they can do on Sales Navigator. The trouble is that LinkedIn does not sell it, and it does not market it very well at all. So that's our job: to go around evangelising about how to use LinkedIn. LinkedIn won't do it, so we have to do it for them.

Radio Host: You and I are connected through LinkedIn, which is quite fortuitous. So, this interview is a great example of the work you do and the power of LinkedIn because had it not been for LinkedIn and had you not started a conversation with me, we would not be talking right now. If you think about your own professional profile, what are you looking to improve for yourself right now?

You must be looking at yourself all the time and thinking, 'Actually, I think I could do that better'. Is there any area that you're improving on your profile right now?

Chris: Of course, every single day. I'm critical of my profile every single day. I change something about my profile all the time, change my headline, I change my picture, I change my background picture. I change the blogging, I change key words, and I change my groups and change my skills every single day. LinkedIn also recently rolled out and changed into a new platform. That means you have to look at it in different and creative ways because the way it looks on the mobile is different to the way it looks on the laptop and the tablet. So, I am constantly looking at how you can maximise it, and I am still learning about it.

I test to see whether certain things work, and then I pass that experience onto my team, and then they pass that experience onto our clients. So, I am very much the test bed of how to use LinkedIn in Asia for Black Marketing and across the world for Black Marketing because we're using it more than anybody else does. I mean, I'm literally on it 24/7. My team are on my profile 24/7, and we're using it and testing it. I'm always critical of my profile. I always think I can do something better on my profile. I'm always trying to increase the rankings of my profile. But as long as I beat the managing director of LinkedIn who lives in Asia Pacific, which I do every single day for the last six years, then I am happy.

I manage it because I believe in the platform and I engage and I'm passionate about it, but I use it and they don't use it. I mean, people who sell LinkedIn here in Sydney and in Hong Kong and Singapore do not use the actual platform. And that's why they don't know half the things that are actually going on. And I tell them things that they should really know, and I'm really surprised they don't know things about their platform. So, it's actually amazing that they're selling it, but they are not using it. So, it's very important that I remain critical of my own profile.

Radio Host: What's the average amount of time that you spend on LinkedIn per day?

Chris: 23 hours {laughs}

Radio Host: Do you dip in and out? Do you have a time where you go, 'I'm going to dig in now and do a half an hour or an hour on LinkedIn for my profile', or do you dip in and out? Do you find you're better at nighttime, or is it the last thing you do? Do you have a ritual around it? Are there habits you have with it, or is it just spontaneous?

Chris: It is every single minute of every single day. I'm not joking. Every single minute, I get my team to work the same thing. So, my team works every single minute of their days on my LinkedIn profile, on their LinkedIn profiles, and also my clients' LinkedIn profiles. But, I'm on it all the time: When I'm watching football and when I am listening to music, I'm on my LinkedIn.

If I am at a concert or on a plane, I am still on my LinkedIn. Literally every single moment of every single day, I am on my LinkedIn, improving it, connecting, and sharing, because I've got 55,000 followers, and I've got engagement going on all the time. So, I've got three other people on my account who work on my accounts. There's basically four of us. It's five hours for each of us working on my account every single day.

So, they're making it active, they're making it lively, they're engaging, they're thanking people, they're accepting people, they're sending out messages to people, and they are basically helping me to build the business because it is a business through my profile, just like Richard Branson's business is basically through his profile online. Richard Branson is a great example because he's got 10 million followers on LinkedIn and Virgin Atlantic and around maybe 100,000 followers.

Virgin Mobile Australia has 9,000 followers. Virgin Active has 50,000 followers. No one follows the company pages. They all follow his profile because he has a positive impact on his Virgin brands. And that's what I do for Black Marketing. I basically leverage Black Marketing by using my brand to drive it forward. So, I have to be at the top of my game. I can't go home on a Friday night and not answer someone's message or not respond to somebody and not participate in a debate that's going on maybe in America or Europe. I don't view time as being time, such as the weekend.

I view time as being people who are on social media 24/7. I have clients here in Australia. I have clients in New Zealand, I have clients in Europe, and I have clients in America. I have clients in Singapore across all these different time zones, which means that there's always something going on with LinkedIn. So, it is not a question of when I am on it; it's more a question of 'When am I not on it?'

Radio Host: Not everybody is going to immerse themselves as Chris J. Reed does. I think that somebody saw you speak in Sydney today. They walked out of the gig and said, 'I am into it. I really like this guy. I'm getting a Mohawk. I'm going to make it orange to distinguish my brand because I don't want to be confused with Chris J. Reed's'.

They are going home, and they have life responsibilities. That person says, 'Chris. I am a disciple. I'm going to start writing'. How much time would you say to that person that they need to spend to start building their own thought leadership on LinkedIn? Just give them some idea of the minimum amount of time that they would need to spend.

Chris: I think you need to spend at least half an hour to an hour a day. But, then you have to take time to actually write your blogs or revamp your summary section, update key words, and source a good picture. You have to spend time thinking about your brand. You need to put thought into the pictures you use, the photographs you use, the videos and the slideshows that you use, and the blogs take the longest time because you have to spend a bit of time researching, thinking about it, writing it, and adding content, but I would say half an hour a day, five days per week is enough time to have an engaging profile.

It doesn't take a lot; it just takes a bit, and LinkedIn start rewarding you with that because they basically reward people who start having a go, and it's a gamification platform. The more you do it, the more they are reward you with the status of higher rankings, so it's just about you basically having a go.

Radio Host: Do you have your own downtime where you basically change gears, and you do deep work because Cal Newport wrote a book called *Deep Work*, which involves you focusing on one thing where you limit distractions and you really immerse yourself in that one thing that has to challenge you slightly?

Chris: No. The quietest time I ever get is on a plane, like last night. I'm on a plane. I'm in the business lounge. You know, I've got the champagne, I've got the sexy Singapore stewardesses, and that's my downtime. But I write my best blogs when I am in a plane with champagne and trance music in my ears. And literally, that's my only downtime.

Radio Host: Where's LinkedIn going? What do we get to see in the next three to five years? Where are they taking it? Where could it go to?

Chris: Excellent question. But three to five years? No one can even predict what is going to happen in six to twelve months. Microsoft has just taken it over, so Microsoft has just spent 26 billion US dollars on LinkedIn, and they need to get their money back. They're going to see a lot of changes in the next couple of years on LinkedIn. I've got great hopes for Microsoft to really transform LinkedIn and to make it fantastic.

And I hope they do it because at the moment there are lots of things that I love about it, but there are a lot of things I hate about it as well. For instance, I have five different accounts under my account, yet none of my inboxes talk to each other. So, I'm hoping that Microsoft come in with their Outlook experience and their seamless Office experience and actually say, 'This is ridiculous'.

People just want to log into one thing with one inbox and have all their mail in one place and have the ability to look at one profile to see whether you contacted them via Recruiter or Premium or Sales Navigator because at the moment, you can't tell. You have to literally check every single platform to see whether you've talked to this person or recruiter, so there is a risk you will end up messaging the same person three times. I'm really hoping Microsoft look at this kind of thing.

It's just a confusing thing about LinkedIn that you don't have three platforms connected to your one account, and the problem is that I have to log in and log out to basically find each of these platforms.

Chapter Ten

How a Personal Branding Strategy Can Make You a Better CEO

Two interesting surveys I recently read lend credence to investment in CEOs who have strong and charismatic personalities in preference to financially-driven company leaders.

Research conducted among 1,500 US bank CEOs found that only 4% of the variation in their performance was accounted for by remuneration. The ten-year study found that in 72% of cases, 'style' trumped pay in determining the success and innovativeness of a bank. Style referred to personality, style, and work ethic: in other words, a personal brand.

This, of course, goes completely against conventional wisdom that dictates the more you pay, the better the leader. The research was conducted by US, UK, and German academics from the NYU's Stern School of Business and Leeds University Business School, who investigated 165 US banks.

Other research was conducted to investigate the best way to measure a CEO's success. The results showed that the CEOs who were paid the most were not necessarily the same as those who most enhanced the value of their company. These results are not to be confused with shareholder value, which can go up and down due to various uncontrollable variables. For instance, shareholder value can also go up as a CEO runs a company into the ground through cost-cutting. Accordingly, the value of a company is directly linked to the CEO's leadership.

The New York Times asked respected consultants to look at a return on capital rather than shareholder value. They thought this was a more accurate reflection of a CEO's worth than their pay and the company's performance. For each of these consultants, *The New York Times* looked at the last 5 years of return on capital, then compared this to that of their peers from the same industry.

The study showed that 74 of the 200 companies that were surveyed overpaid their CEO when looking at a 5-year capital return that compared CEOs with their peers. Sectors who overpaid the most were media, consumer goods, health, technology, and energy. Among these were SalesForce.com and Vertex Pharmaceuticals.

Interestingly, the survey also showed that there was a similar number of CEOs who were underpaid or who were paid approximately the right amount as determined by their capital investment over the last 5 years. This included MasterCard and Philip Morris.

So what do you think of these two metrics? How do you value your leader? If you are a CEO, how do you measure your own performance most accurately? How do outside viewers of your company measure your performance? What matters most to your shareholders?

I am part of The Marketing Group Plc, which recently floated on NASDAQ. The photo shown was the afternoon of our float, and I couldn't wish to have more colourful and charismatic CEOs as my fellow founding companies: Ross from Nice and Polite; Aghir of Creative Insurgeance; Laurent of One9Ninety, with a little help from the equally charismatic Callum Laing in the background; and of course, Jeremy Harbour.

Their infectious personalities beat anything else for me: Their personal brands are strong, distinct, engaging, and ambitious. Paying any of us more wouldn't make us better CEOs because we are already inspired, driven entrepreneurs. It's not about the money; it's a passion and a mission. The money comes if you lead your company through the fires and brickbats with strength, charisma, and a powerful personal brand.

Chapter Eleven

What You Wear Expresses Your Personal Brand

Do clothes still maketh the man (and woman!)?

For the uninitiated, our office is predominantly women. By mainly, I mean 95%.

The CEO, Chris J. Reed, has a red Mohawk and is allergic to suits.

I admit; I am the catalyst. This debate first started when I made a flippant comment from my little corner of the office a number of years ago when I was working for someone else.

On looking up, I saw a candidate walk in wearing a sheer, black lace top that was see-through in the back, with a bodycon skirt. Mind you, she was an attractive girl, and she carried off the look. There was nothing wrong with the outfit per se. Nevertheless, my gripe and immediate comment when I realised what she was here for was 'Who wears clubbing clothes to an interview?'

My comment apparently surprised my boss at the time because I myself am not exactly what you would call a conservative dresser. He pointed out that sometimes, I too, wear clothes that travel quite comfortably from the boardroom to the bar. To which I retorted, 'Yes, but never to an interview'.

I understand that the modern corporate world, mixed with the fickle world of fashion, has changed the rules about what's appropriate to wear in the office. This is particularly so in the creative industries. These days, there are even places where shorts and flip-flops are the style du jour. And at Black Marketing, one of the ways I try to cultivate creativity is to allow my staff to express themselves freely through dress.

My stance is: If you are not meeting anyone, then I don't see why you have to wear anything that you would not feel good about yourself in. In fact, if you are meeting someone, they are buying our services, our brains, our know-how, our experience, and our ability to save them time. They tend to be entrepreneurs, so they don't tend to care how you are dressed. Go sexy, go conservative, or go the way you feel on that day. Provided your freedom to dress however you please makes you a better Black Marketing professional when you meet a client or when you're just in the office, the principle applies.

I am not going to lie. In theory, the principle is sound. As I mentioned earlier, I understand that the lines when it comes to suitable corporate attire have been blurred these days. Nevertheless, I stand by my somewhat critical comment about the female job candidate who wore a see-through top and bodycon skirt because, at the end of the day, the rules for an interview and the psychology of forming an opinion of a person when you first meet them haven't really changed. Your aim in an interview is to impress the interviewer and have them form the best opinion of you in their evaluation. So as superficial as it sounds, looks do play a part.

'Whether you like it or not, your appearance is the first thing people notice about you, and first impressions are usually formed within the first 30 seconds', says Brenda Ferguson Hodges, a California-based image consultant and career coach. 'Appearance affects hiring decisions and plays a major role. Hiring managers need to be able to visualise you in the position they are trying to fill'.

So what's my point in all of this? Nothing really, other than that I stand by my comment whilst I continue to fully enjoy the perks of being in Black Marketing (with creative dressing and crazy-coloured hair!). But let's face it, beyond the experience, I got here because I dressed appropriately for my interviews in the past.

This discussion has raised other questions for me, more out of curiosity and a genuine interest in the human psyche than anything else. But my biggest question is: Had the girl not been attractive or overweight in the same clothes, would we be having this conversation, or would she have been examined, head to toe, then dismissed as unsuitable? Be honest.

So my two cents on this is that you can wear whatever you want, whatever you think is appropriate for the person you are meeting, or the environment that you work in. I tell my team that when they're at the office, provided they are not meeting anyone, then there's no need for them to wear anything that they would not feel good in. Similarly, if they are meeting someone who is buying our services, our brains, our know-how, our experience and our ability to save them time, the way they dress hardly matters then either.

I don't dress differently to meet a CEO, conduct an interview, or to lead a team event. The only time I wear a jacket is for speaking/ events and half the time that comes off because I find that no one cares what I wear. If I do wear a jacket, it's more to carry my business cards and the ones I collect around with me! Plus, they tend to be funky jackets anyway!

When I worked at *The Times* in 1990s, I wore a striped suit, waistcoat, and tie, and it made no difference. It was more about my confidence in dealing with the top people at News Corp than anything else: super powerful editors and executives who all went to Oxbridge (needless to say, I did not!).

Now, I don't care, and I have the confidence, the credibility, and the experience. If people don't like it, then I won't be untrue to myself in order to win business. It's always been much more of a talking point and a positive than it has ever been negative. No one has ever not bought our services because of my Mohawk or because of me not wearing a suit. In fact, the reverse is true.

My unique personal branding means that I am recognised at any event, any bar, and any restaurant in Singapore. So, I tell my team to dress how they please, to express themselves, get noticed, remind people who we are, stand out, and make a difference. What we do is unique, and we continually gain more clients because our brand is different, which is reflected in the way each of us dresses.

Express yourself. I give my staff the ultimate employee benefits: We pay for them to dye their hair, but it has to be a unique and cool colour. I told my team to go purple, go blue, go red, go green. I told them they have the power to stand out, and in doing so, they have further inspiration to create something truly unique for our current and future clients.

In conclusion, while I concede that the clothes no longer maketh the man or woman, appearances nevertheless do continue to significantly influence people's perception of you. 'Clothes make the man. Naked people have little or no influence on society', explained Mark Twain.

Chapter Twelve
Richard Branson and Personal Branding

Richard Branson's personal brand is 100 times more powerful than the Virgin one. Here's why:

Richard Branson has 13 million followers on LinkedIn, which renders him the number one most followed professional on LinkedIn by far. His personal brand is so powerful that he showers glitter and gold over every single Virgin brand because of his iconic entrepreneurial status.

If you ask any professional on LinkedIn who is exposed to his numerous LinkedIn blog posts, the majority will say that Virgin is a cool, fun place to work, and that the brand is one of the most entrepreneurial. Remove Branson from the equation, and the picture is the same as any other airline, mobile, financial, or fitness brand: nothing special.

That's the power of Branson's personal brand and the power of content marketing on LinkedIn. It works. Branson recently came to Singapore to do a talk and much of the talk was about how he uses his personal brand to market the Virgin empire of brands.

The picture says it all: Branson is wearing a Virgin Active t-shirt, with the iconic Singapore skyline in the background as he promotes the opening of the new gym.

But the loyalty stops there. At Branson. It's his personal brand that is carrying the company and all of its myriad of brands: like Steve Jobs and Elon Musk (Jobs less so long-term, but Elon Musk is intrinsically tied to Space X and Tesla, like Branson is to Virgin Atlantic and Virgin Mobile). Musk even manages it without being on LinkedIn. Perhaps, LinkedIn's new owners, Microsoft, should ask him.

People relate to people. People buy people. People have always liked Branson's PR stunts from when he took on British Airways with a couple of planes and some clever stunts in the 1980s, or when he created Virgin Records from nothing, yet managed to compete with the big guns. The same was the case with Virgin Mobile, Virgin Money, and many others.

Everyone loves the David and Goliath story. Of course, ironically, now he's the Goliath, and there are many Davids snapping at his heels. This is why he has gone into overdrive on platforms like LinkedIn—to create a compelling content marketing and branding campaign.

Branson is also a very frequent book writer. Search Amazon for his books, and there are many, all very contrived and full of very positive advice, just like his blogs. There are many more that feature him, at least in part. It's all part of the personal branding strategy.

Ironically, he reaches more people through blogging on LinkedIn than he ever could in book form, but the books give him another avenue and credibility. Just like his talks, it's all part of his overall strategy of putting himself out there, so that he will be seen as a thought leader. Just doing it enhances his personal brand.

In one of his many blogs on Virgin.com, Branson makes the point that many entrepreneurs are actually introverts. He admits himself that he is very much an introvert. However, he adopted a more extroverted persona in the interests of enhancing his personal brand and to elevate his company brand. Every leader of industry, company owner, CEO, and entrepreneur should be inspired by this, if by nothing else about him.

Many of Branson's brands have disappeared when it transpired that Branson's fairy dust really didn't stretch to things like Brides and Cinemas, to name just two failed ventures. You can't polish crap, as the saying goes.

The Virgin space mission, Galactic, is all about transforming the Virgin brand to the next level, and communicating the Virgin brand is as much as it is about selling tickets to the moon. This is something Elon Musk realised quite early with his trip to Mars plan, designed to position Space X in a similar way. He is a clever man who learned from the master, then went one better. It doesn't matter that he may not achieve it; it's the fact that it is his big dream, and people love to buy into unrealistic dreams that they will never be part of or benefit from.

Branson is very clever in the way he structures his blogs on LinkedIn: He is an always happy, smiling Richard, always Richard in amongst the masses, the teams, and the people. The headlines they use are also very sophisticated: Fun. Passion. Work Life Balance. They are all very cleverly done, and people on LinkedIn lap it up.

Branson gets hundreds of thousands of views for each blog, which is free marketing for Virgin. It was a very clever move by LinkedIn to sign him up as their first and most inspirational entrepreneur and official LinkedIn Influencer. No one else comes close. It has benefited Branson as much as it has LinkedIn. A true win-win. They both gain positive brand association from the partnership.

So why is Richard Branson's personal brand worth more than 100 times the Virgin one?

Richard Branson has 13 million followers.

The best performing Virgin company page on LinkedIn only has 100,000 followers: 1% of his followers. It really does hammer home the point that people don't follow and engage with companies on LinkedIn despite being a business platform; instead, they follow and engage with leaders of companies and professionals. They follow and engage with you.

This is worth remembering when you're thinking about your personal branding and company branding marketing strategy on LinkedIn. Focus and invest in the owner, the founder, the leader, the CEO, but not the company. Market the company and its values and initiatives through the leader. Humanise them. Personalise them. Use the power of the personal brand to market the company brand, just like Richard Branson does.

Of course, if you have read either of Tom Bower's unflattering books on the real Richard Branson, you will have a more balanced picture than just taking everything Branson says as gospel. But whatever you think of him, you have to admire his marketing genius in using his personal brand when there was no Internet, and then accentuating it when there was.

Chapter Thirteen

Be Yourself - Billions Shows You How

The American television drama series, *Billions*, reached a gripping and nerve-jangling grand finale in May 2017. I won't spoil anything if you're storing up the episodes to watch them all in one go, but it suffices to say that the twists and turns in the penultimate episode left me on the edge of my seat.

I love many things about this business drama, starring the anti-hero Bobby Axe (Axelrod) as a billionaire hedge fund company owner, entrepreneur, and financial disruptor. One thing that always impressed me is how he demonstrates that you can be yourself, dress as you wish, and still be an entrepreneur, business leader, and company owner.

This is epitomised in *Billions* by what Axe wears. His normal office attire is a rock star t-shirt or a casual t-shirt with trainers. He rarely wears a suit. There are a couple of great demonstrations of this in the latest series where he's about to meet the district attorney and in another scenario when he's there to pitch a client he desperately needs, and he starts contemplating dressing in a suit, tie, and shirt. He looks at himself in the mirror before each meeting, thinks about it, and you can almost see him thinking, 'No, this isn't me. This isn't how I feel comfortable, and how I want to be seen. This isn't how I go into battle. I can't give my best in this'.

He quickly removes the tie and shirt, and changes into his comfortable battle dress of a Megadeath t-shirt and on one occasion, a Metallica one. By doing this, he takes people off guard, and without spoilers, he gets the better of both encounters.

Axe is being true to himself by not dressing how his opponents or convention tells him to. There is another occasion when he walks into a private member's club in trainers, jeans, and a t-shirt, which has the same effect: Surprise, outrage, and he catches his opponents off guard.

Now, you might say that it's alright for him in a fictional sense because he's a billionaire, and he works for himself. You have a point, but even when you are working for yourself, you will still have conventional and conservative clients to deal with, like venture capitalists and banks.

If you dress like everyone else, in a bland corporate suit and blue/white shirt (the banker's uniform), then you will just look like everyone else. Your personal brand is diminished by doing so because you're not standing out and enhancing your brand values. This is fine if you don't wish to stand out, but then don't complain when someone else gets the promotion, pay rise, client, investment, employee, award, recognition, etc.

Be yourself. Even if you do work for someone else, you're an entrepreneur and are being pressured, or you feel that conservatism and convention are telling you to wear a bland suit and shirt/tie for an important investor or client meeting, then ask yourself whether it is really you.

Are you going to give your best if you're dressed in a way that someone else wants you to, or in the manner society wants you to dress rather than dressing the way that you personally feel most comfortable? By being yourself and dressing how you wish, you will be amazed how this will enable you to be yourself, feel more like yourself, and give your best work, free from the chains of conventional restraint.

It's better to be true to yourself and fail than to pretend to be someone else and win. You'll get found out eventually, and you won't be happy. Be yourself and you'll be surprised by how much confidence saying, 'Stuff you, convention!' does for your self-confidence on stage, in front of clients, with your team, in conversation with your peers, networking, and, in fact, anywhere you come into contact with the business community.

Try it. Be yourself.

Chapter Fourteen

The Joker's Top 10 Personal Branding Tips

The Joker, more specifically Heath Ledger's chilling Oscar-winning Joker in *The Dark Knight*, can teach us many things about personal branding. Here are my 10 favourite things that the Joker teaches us:

1. Be yourself.

Like all people who accentuate their personal brands, they are ultimately true to themselves and broadcast their unique qualities and presence to amplify their personal brand on all relevant stages and platforms.

The Joker is very much himself. He walks into a room, down a street, through a ceiling/door, and every single time, you immediately recognise him. The Joker's grasp of theatrics is unmistakable. The Joker's business card caps the performance. Who else's business card makes such an impression?

The Joker walks into a room, and people stop what they're doing and engage. He captures your imagination and attention. Your personal brand should rise above others to communicate your brand values, just like the Joker's does.

If he had a LinkedIn profile, it would be worthwhile looking at and reading his thought leadership. He commands interest, intrigue, and curiosity, and then he delivers. These are excellent personal branding characteristics.

2. Look how you want.

The Joker is a cross between Johnny Rotten and Iggy Pop, Clockwork Orange and various depictions of artistic Hell. The Joker combines the makeup of a clown, with a bright red Glaswegian smile, disconcerting and misdirecting his opponents by constantly smiling whilst spreading chaos and mayhem.

The Joker's long, straggly, green hair accentuates his heavily made-up face. The Joker's purple suit, thin, bright tie, green waistcoat, and blue shirt show a certain style and confidence. This guy doesn't lack self-assurance in how he presents himself or in how he dresses.

No matter what industry you're in, you need to stand out. Even if you're in financial services or the legal profession, you still need to stand out to enhance your personal brand and to achieve your professional goals. You do not necessarily need to achieve this in the same way as the Joker or with a Mohawk, but this principle should be adopted in the context of your industry. So, stripey, colourful shirts, funky designer suits, or quirky shoes are all options. In fact, there are a million ways to stand out.

Adopting this idea is definitely easier for a woman than a man, but nonetheless, anyone who says they can't isn't thinking about their personal branding like the Joker.

3. Disrupt your industry.

One of the Joker's great quotes is 'Introduce a little anarchy, upset the established order, and everything becomes chaos. I'm an agent of chaos'. The Joker is a disruptor. He is looking to disrupt his industry, just as you might be looking at doing in yours.

The Joker uses the strength of his personal branding and his vision to create awareness of the industry he is in. He comes in and disrupts the established order. You can too.

You have greater power and visibility if you do this with a more notable and enhanced personal brand. People pay attention to people who stand out and people who use their personal brand to do so. Change can happen more easily if more people are aware of your disruptive ideas.

4. Value your services.

'If you're good at something, never do it for free' is one of the best quotes from the Joker. It encapsulates everything entrepreneurial about him and his personal brand. He has certain qualities, leadership attributes, and abilities to get things done, so you should pay for this service.

The Joker's forceful personality means that you rarely argue with this reasoning. He also tends to deliver every time he is asked to do something, which enhances his personal branding credentials further. He's the can-do guy to whom you go when you can't do something yourself, or when you don't have the time or resources yourself.

5. Enjoy your work—don't work just for money.

'Everything burns!' the Joker exclaimed when he burned his mountain of cash taken from the Mob. Clearly, The Joker very much enjoys his work. He doesn't do it for the money; the money is just the end that justifies the means, rather than being a desire for wealth in itself.

The Joker's ultimate riposte to the Mob's desire for money is to burn his share and their share at the same time. As he says, 'I'm a man of simple tastes. I like dynamite and gunpowder . . . and gasoline! Do you know what all of these things have in common? They're cheap!'

Do what you do because you love it, have a passion for it, and because you enjoy it, just as the Joker does. These attributes really come across in your personal branding because people can respect and feel your passion for what you do.

7. Focus on your competition and raise your game.

Every business needs competition to raise their game. The best sports managers always create fictional or real competitors to fire up a team and raise their game. This manifests itself in actual face-off matches, but the trick is to maintain this throughout a season to motivate a team that consistently delivers results.

You can only truly lead with this kind of vision and ethos if you have the personal branding, charisma, and reputation to inspire, frighten, and motivate a team to focus on this mission and deliver.

The Joker has Batman in his clutches. It defines him. As he says, 'You just couldn't let me go, could you? This is what happens when an unstoppable force meets an immovable object. You won't kill me out of some misplaced sense of self-righteousness. And I won't kill you because you're just too much fun. I think you and I are destined to do this forever . . . '.

'You complete me', the Joker tells Batman. Like Apple without Samsung, Coke without Pepsi, Nike without Adidas, or Microsoft without Google, you need an enemy to focus on, and you need a competitor to focus your team on.

8) Lead by example and create competition to follow you.

'Now, our operation is small, but there is a lot of potential for "aggressive" expansion. So which one of you, fine gentlemen, would like to join our team? Oh, there's only one spot open right now, so we're gonna have . . . ', says the Joker on a recruitment drive.

Everyone wants to work for a Richard Branson, Elon Musk, or a one-off genius (except not for a terrible boss, like Steve Jobs). Well, everyone does until reality bites. But by that stage, you have worked for them, learned things about the business, leadership, and the reality that you do/don't like, and you either adapt to the environment or leave and become a better, more rounded leader yourself.

People work for people just like people buy from people. Personal branding is intrinsically linked to your leadership credentials and kudos.

9. Have a personal branding ethos.

'I believe that whatever doesn't kill you makes you stranger'. This is the Joker's personal branding strap-line, the way he defines himself, and it's his constant internal and external branding. He pushes his personal brand to the limits and becomes stronger and stronger the more he pushes those boundaries. This, in turn, accentuates his personal branding.

People are stimulated by someone else's personal brand ethos, and whether the branding ethos is negative or positive, it creates a reaction. What is yours? What is your personal branding strap-line? What encapsulates what you believe and how you behave?

10. Your personal brand should be based on personal experience.

'Why so serious?' Every personal brand needs to be based on reality, experience, and personal happenings in your life. The Joker tells the story of how he got the scars across his mouth in several different ways, usually due to his father's abuse or to placate his wife. It's personal. But it manifests itself in his personal brand.

His ever-present Glaswegian smile is intrinsic to his personal brand. It's what defines him and makes him stand out. No one else has a physical feature that communicates their personal brand in quite the same way as the Joker's scarred, ever-present smile. He endured living with a scarred face every day, but his face morphed into something positive that enabled him to use it as his personal brand signature, a point of difference, icebreaker, or USP.

Your personal brand is defined by your personal experience. Live it, breathe it, communicate it. You too can have a personal brand in your professional context, just as the Joker has his in his professional environment!

Chapter Fifteen

Breaking Bad's Top 10 Personal Branding Tips

Breaking Bad's Heisenberg has given us some amazing personal branding tips. Here are my top 10 favourites:

1. Know the power of your personal brand.

One of my favourite lines of any character in any TV series is when Walter White (who by this stage is very much drug warlord, Heisenberg) declares to his rivals in the middle of the desert (after just blowing away the Mafia and his rival, sho he is now the undisputed king of drugs), 'Say my name. Say it. Say my name'. 'Heisenberg' is the trembling answer. King of all he surveys!

This is a brilliant moment that marks the journey that Walter has taken from nerd and part-time drug creator to mega drug dealer and full-on, feared gangster. The power of the personal brand of Heisenberg has overwhelmed anything else he was before, and he wants everyone to know who he is.

2. Build a business in your personal brand.

Early on in *Breaking Bad*, Walter White realises that he can't use 'Walter White' as a drug lord name because it doesn't really put fear into your heart. So, he creates the mythical alter-ego name of Heisenberg. Heisenberg resonates a personal brand of intensity and fear.

It's a reference to German physicist, Werner Heisenberg, famous for his uncertainty principle, which states that the exact position and momentum of a particle cannot be simultaneously known. On a deeper level, the name symbolises Walter's Jekyll-and-Hyde transition from weak chemistry teacher to feared drug lord.

Walter can, therefore, be viewed as a human manifestation of the uncertainty principle: As he gains momentum as a murderous drug lord, he loses sight of his original position as a family man with a strong moral code.

The personal brand that the business is founded on is Heisenberg. Walter lives that personal brand in order to do business in that context.

3. Dress to match your personal brand.

When Walter puts on his black pork-pie hat and black trench coat, he becomes Heisenberg. He is then able to commit hideous murderous acts that the regular, down-to-earth Walter would never be capable of. It's a form of psychological departmentalisation that lets Walter distance himself from his evil acts and convince himself that he's still a good person.

Walter wears the uniform of the personal brand that he has created. That is very much part of his personal branding. It is also the symbol everyone associates with *Breaking Bad*.

4. Know your competition and deal with them.

Walter also had more notorious and often aggressive partners/enemies, the most infamous being Gus Fring. A partner to start with, Gus turned into an enemy who didn't last long after that. Heisenberg took on the Mafia, his own brother-in-law who was a DEA agent, the FBI, and anyone who got in his way.

The personal brand of Heisenberg sought out and dealt with all manner of competition in every way you can imagine. It dealt with them in ways that science teacher, Walter White, simply wouldn't.

Just like the Joker or Batman enabled those people to do good/evil by wearing makeup/costumes, Walter White turned into Heisenberg when he needed to operate as the drug lord and ruthless businessman, Heisenberg. The effect was the same, especially because, unlike Bruce Wayne/Batman, people who came across him did not know him as the Walter White personal brand; they only knew him as the ruthless, not to be messed with Heisenberg.

5. You need partners to build your business.

No matter how strong your personal brand is, you can't do it alone. Whether you are Richard Branson or Heisenberg, you need partners to build on your personal brand. In *Breaking Bad*, Walter had Jesse, who was a willing, somewhat scattered, and comical sidekick.

Heisenberg and Jesse were chalk and cheese, but they both bought into the business. More importantly, Jesse realised that it was Walter's imagination, technical know-how, and personal brand (in the form of the alter ego, Heisenberg) that built and continued to build the business that he benefited from.

6. 'Stay out of my territory'.

Another great quote from Breaking Bad is when the now fully formed and fully menacing Heisenberg sees some potential competition and lets them know in no uncertain terms that this is his business territory. His personal brand by now is so menacing and all-consuming that these hardened criminals scoot away from him as far as possible.

The personal brand that Heisenberg has developed has given him so much confidence as to enable him to do things he would never have dreamt of doing before. Personal branding himself has allowed him to delve deeply into his inner darkness and use that to achieve his business objectives. No one was going to take his territory away from him; this was what he had worked for and made sacrifices for, and no one was going to get in his way.

7. 'I am the one who knocks'.

This is probably the most famous and iconic quote from *Breaking Bad*, and it is a quote that really sums up how far Walter has come in terms of his transformation into Heisenberg. He used to be the one who cowered, but now he is the one who knocks to frighten and kill. No more on the other side of door, he is the one banging on doors to intimidate and frighten his competition and anyone who gets in his way.

Heisenberg's personal brand is now full of confidence. His brand is now the one that goes around making things happen. It's a lesson in how the strength of a personal brand can give someone the powerful inner belief and focus that they were missing before. You too can make something happen, you too can ensure that you are being proactive and not reactive, and you too can be the one who knocks!

8. Don't let fear stop you.

Personal branding can be a holistic way to give every aspect of your life confidence to move forward. Fear is the number one reason why people don't do anything.

In *Breaking Bad*, Heisenberg has an answer to this to ensure that his personal brand is fearless. The quote goes, 'What I came to realise is that fear is the worst of it; that's the real enemy. So get up, get out in the real world, and you kick that bastard as hard as you can right in the teeth'.

9. 'I'm not in the meth business; I'm in the empire business'.

Having been short-changed in his original company, Grey Matter, and then selling his stake for five thousand dollars (which then turned out to be worth hundreds of millions), Walter has vengeance and a determination to recoup everything that he believes should have been his. This was after he and Jesse made five million dollars each from some deals. Jesse was happy, but Walter was not.

Walter had a long way to go. He had a goal, a vision, and a driving force to build an empire. He was not in the meth business; he was in the empire business.

Everyone with a personal brand needs to have an objective. What is your personal brand achieving? What is your long-term vision? What is the empire that you are building with it?

10. 'Tread lightly'; do your research.

Heisenberg utters this line to his brother-in-law and DEA leader, Hank when Hank finally realises what has been staring him the face for several years: that the drug lord he has been after for all of that time is Walter, his own brother-in-law.

Walter relishes this as Hank has always looked down on him and underestimated him, and all this time Walter/Heisenberg has been running rings around him, building a drug empire business worth hundreds of millions of dollars.

In terms of personal branding, there are two lessons here:

1) Don't assume/underestimate someone's personal brand just because they don't tell you everything about themselves. There will always be aspects of their personal brand that they may not wish you to know about/keep secret/have a darker personal brand elsewhere.

2) Do your research on who you are working with on their personal brand, or at least research their public personal brand. Everything is out there, and it is up to you to find it. There are no excuses for not knowing about someone's personal brand before you meet them. You never know: You could be meeting the next Heisenberg.

Chapter Sixteen

American Psycho's Top 10 Personal Branding Tips

American Psycho is one of my favourite films, and it's amazing at giving personal branding tips that you can follow (or completely ignore, but they're fun to think about!). Here are my top 10 tips from the film that you seriously need to consider to enhance your personal brand, whether you're a serial killer or not!

Please beware that if you are easily offended, you may not enjoy this chapter because it includes some uncensored content, including violence. You have been warned!

1. Your business card

American Psycho explores the status of your personal brand as it is manifested through the quality of business cards and that of their competitors at Pierce and Pierce.

The card is a symbol. It's all about what the card says about that person's personal brand. It's amazing, but even in the Digital Age, people are still using business cards despite everything being online or on LinkedIn. There is still a kudos/personal brand statement that people communicate via their business card.

The quality of your business card still says a lot about you and your personal brand. As my business card I personally now just use my #1 international best-selling book, *LinkedIn Mastery for Entrepreneurs*, because it's about the same price as one of those embossed, watermarked cards in American Psycho. Also, it doesn't get lost in terms of enhancing my personal brand. In my view, my book is more memorable.

The dialogue about the business card competition between the film's main characters is very droll and funny:

Bateman: New card. What do you think?

McDermott: Whoa-ho, very nice. Look at that.

Bateman: Picked them up from the printer's yesterday.

Van Patten: Good colouring.

Bateman: That's 'Bone'. And the lettering is something called 'Silian Rail'.

Van Patten: It's very cool, Bateman . . . but that's nothing. Look at this.

{Van Patten removes his card from its holder.}

Bryce: That is really nice.

Van Patten: 'Eggshell', with 'Ramalian' type. What do you think?

Bateman: . . . Nice.

Bryce: Jesus. That is really super. How'd a nitwit like you get so tasteful?

Bateman {internal monologue}: I can't believe that Bryce prefers Van Patten's card to mine.

Bryce: But wait, you ain't seen nothing yet.

{Bryce removes his card from its holder.}

Bryce: Raised lettering, 'Pale Nimbus'. White.

Bateman: Impressive. Very nice. . . . Let's see Paul Allen's card.

{Bryce slowly reveals Paul Allen's card.}

Bateman {internal monologue}: Look at that subtle off-white coloring. The tasteful thickness of it. Oh my God, it even has a watermark.

{Bateman seethes.}

Carruthers: Something wrong? . . . Patrick? You're sweating.

2. Your musical tastes

Liking Phil Collins, Chris De Burgh, Whitney Houston, and Huey Lewis and the News, even back in the 1980s, wasn't something to be admired or admitted, but to introduce any or all of them into daily work conversations would definitely set your personal brand back. If you also do so whilst entertaining escorts, your personal brand may be beyond saving (as the following film conversation clearly shows).

{To two prostitutes} Do you like Phil Collins?

I've been a big Genesis fan ever since the release of their 1980 album, *Duke*. Before that, I really didn't understand any of their work. Too artsy, too intellectual. It was on *Duke* where, uh, Phil Collins' presence became more apparent.

I think 'Invisible Touch' was the group's undisputed masterpiece. It's an epic meditation on intangibility. At the same time, it deepens and enriches the meaning of the preceding three albums.

Listen to the brilliant ensemble playing of Banks, Collins, and Rutherford. You can practically hear every nuance of every instrument. In terms of lyrical craftsmanship, the sheer songwriting, this album hits a new peak of professionalism.

Take the lyrics to 'Land of Confusion'. In this song, Phil Collins addresses the problems of abusive political authority. 'In Too Deep' is the most moving pop song of the 1980s about monogamy and commitment. The song is extremely uplifting. Their lyrics are as positive and affirmative as, uh, anything I've heard in rock.

Phil Collins' solo career seems to be more commercial and, therefore, more satisfying, in a narrower way. Especially songs like 'In the Air Tonight' and, uh, 'Against All Odds'.

But I also think Phil Collins works best within the confines of the group than as a solo artist, and I stress the word artist. This is 'Sussudio', a great, great song, a personal favourite'. {End of excerpt}

Clearly, this is NOT enhancing to your personal brand.

3. Your cleansing/fitness regime

Your personal grooming is very important to your personal brand. This especially applies when going from online to offline. If you have an enhanced personal brand online, and then it disappoints offline, you only have yourself to blame. You can always follow Patrick's personal grooming regime to enhance your personal brand's physical characteristics too. Here's the scene from the film:

I live in the American Gardens Building on West 81st Street on the 11th floor.

My name is Patrick Bateman. I'm 27 years old.

I believe in taking care of myself, and I maintain a balanced diet and a rigorous exercise routine. In the morning, if my face is a little puffy, I'll put on an ice pack while doing my stomach crunches. I can do a thousand now.

After I remove the ice pack, I use a deep pore cleansing lotion. In the shower I use a water-activated gel cleanser, then a honey almond body scrub, and on the face, I use an exfoliating gel scrub.

Then I apply a herb-mint facial masque that I leave on for 10 minutes while I prepare the rest of my routine. I always use an aftershave lotion with little or no alcohol because alcohol dries your face out and makes you look older.

Then I use moisturiser, then an anti-ageing eye balm, followed by a final moisturising protective lotion.

There is an idea of a Patrick Bateman. Some kind of abstraction. But there is no real me. Only an entity. Something illusory. And though I can hide my cold gaze, and you can shake my hand and feel flesh gripping yours, and maybe you can even sense our lifestyles are probably comparable, I am simply not there.

4. Your concern about world events

Clearly, to enhance your personal brand you need to care about world events; it's very accentuating to your personal branding, just as the following dialogue demonstrates:

Bateman: Come on, Bryce. There are a lot more important problems than Sri Lanka to worry about.

Bryce: Like what?

Bateman: Well, we have to end apartheid for one. And slow down the nuclear arms race, stop terrorism and world hunger. We have to provide food and shelter for the homeless, and oppose racial discrimination and promote civil rights while also promoting equal rights for women. We have to encourage a return to traditional moral values. Most importantly, we have to promote general social concern and encourage less materialism in young people.

It's very admirable and always good to include some non-profit work in your personal brand.

5. Your suits/dress sense

Two of my favourite film posters from *American Psycho* marketed the film with two impactful and memorable personal branding lines: 'No introductions necessary' and 'Killer looks'. Both get to the heart of the film and are the key to personal branding.

If people know who you are, and they understand what your personal brand represents in a positive/memorable way without an introduction, then that is the ultimate in accentuating your personal brand.

Clearly, you don't need to go to the lengths Patrick went to in order to get that kind of recognition and fulfilment, but the lessons are there from the story.

6. Your girlfriend/boyfriend

Clearly, your choice of girlfriend/boyfriend in the 1980s said something about your personal brand, and in some circles, it still does today. You are the company you keep.

Do look out for those people who break up with this quote . . .

Bateman: I don't think we should see each other any more.

Evelyn: Why? What's wrong?

Bateman: My need to engage in homicidal behaviour on a massive scale cannot be corrected.

Not much can be added to this statement apart from an instruction to run away as fast and as far as possible, without wasting time to check whether your ex is following you with a chainsaw.

More seriously, the company you keep clearly says much about your personal brand. Patrick spent most of his life killing homeless people, rivals, or prostitutes (after having sex with them). He also imagined doing so to his disliked arrogant partners from his firm, Pierce and Pierce. He fantasised about a similar fate for bankers/lawyers/brokers from similar Wall Street firms whose personal branding always centred around who they knew (alongside their business cards, of course).

7. Your work

Love your work to enhance your personal brand. Now, your work (as in Patrick's case) may not be your day job . . .

Bateman: Ask me a question.

Club Girl: So, what do you do?

Bateman: I'm into, uh, well, murders and executions, mostly.

Club girl: Do you like it?

Bateman: Well, it depends. Why?

Club Girl: Well, most guys I know who are in mergers and acquisitions really don't like it.

Bateman has a different kind of merger and acquisition that may lead to your head being chopped off and displayed in the fridge . . .

Your work, though, is personal brand enhancing. Patrick didn't enjoy his, he was never there, and when he was there, he listened to terrible 1980's music and read books.

Your work is part of your personal brand. Therefore, possessing outside interests, being a non-exec director, working for non-profit organisations, and putting back into the community are all personal brand enhancing.

8. Your friends/associates

It is best not to mention Huey Lewis and the News around psychopaths, or indeed even comment about the fact that they are wearing raincoats indoors; they don't react very well to their personal brand being challenged in such ways . . .

Bateman: You like Huey Lewis and the News?

Paul Allen: They're OK.

Bateman: Their early work was a little too New Wave for my tastes, but when Sports came out in 1983, I think they really came into their own, commercially and artistically. The whole album has a clear, crisp sound, and a new sheen of consummate professionalism that really gives the songs a big boost. He has been compared to Elvis Costello, but I think Huey has a far more bitter, cynical sense of humour.

Paul Allen: Hey, Halberstram.

Bateman: Yes, Allen?

Paul Allen: Why are there copies of the style section all over the place, d-do you have a dog? A little chow or something?

Bateman: No, Allen.

Paul Allen: Is that a rain coat?

Bateman: Yes it is! In 1987, Huey released this, *Fore!*, their most accomplished album. I think their undisputed masterpiece is 'Hip to Be Square', a song so catchy that most people probably don't listen to the lyrics. {rapidly, as if agitated} But they should, because it's not just about the pleasures of conformity and the importance of trends, it's also a personal statement about the band itself. {raises axe above head} Hey, Paul!

{He bashes Allen in the head with the axe and blood splatters over him.}

Bateman: TRY GETTING A RESERVATION AT DORSIA NOW YOU STUPID IDIOT!

Envy is a terrible thing when it comes to admiring someone else's personal brand. Develop your own so that you're happy with it rather than take out your frustrations on someone who has one that appears better than yours.

9. Your level of honesty

In one of the most memorable scenes of *American Psycho*, Patrick decides to confess on an old-fashioned answer phone. This is not personal brand enhancing and is to be avoided at all costs, especially if you're a psychotic serial killer:

Howard! It's Bateman, Patrick Bateman. You're my lawyer, so I think you should know I've killed a lot of people. Some escort girls in an apartment uptown . . . uh . . . some homeless people, maybe five or ten. Uh . . .

Some NYU girl I met in Central Park; I left her in a parking lot behind some doughnut shop. I killed Bethany, my old girlfriend, with a nail gun and . . . some man, some old gay with a dog. Last week, I killed another girl . . . with a chainsaw . . . I had to, she almost got away. And there . . . was someone else there I don't remember, maybe a model, but sh- she's dead, too.

And, uh- PAUL ALLEN! I killed Paul Allen with an axe! In the face! His body is dissolving in a bathtub in Hell's Kitchen! I don't want to leave anything out here—I guess I've killed maybe . . . 20 people . . . maybe 40! Uh-huh-huh—I have uh . . . tapes of a lot of it.

Some of the girls have seen the tapes—I even . . . I ate some of their brains, and I tried to cook a little. Tonight, I uh—just had to kill a lot of people! And I'm not sure I'm gonna get away with it . . . this time. I mean . . .

I mean, I guess I'm a pretty sick guy. So, if you get back tomorrow, I may show up at Harry's Bar.

So, you know, keep your eyes OPEN. OK, bye. {End of excerpt}

Polite to the end.

Honesty in your personal brand is key though. Don't create parts of your personal brand that are not true to yourself and don't stack up; otherwise, they become negative personal brand values.

Be less Asian/English/Australian/New Zealander and have faith in what you have done and talk about your achievements. If you don't, there will be some American who comes along who will do it because they at least do comprehend the need for self-promotion . . . although you could argue that they take it way too far the other way.

A balance between cultures and how these manifest themselves in eloquently communicating your personal brand is key for sincerity, to be taken seriously, and to receive empathy.

Also, when making excuses about leaving a situation, you must be sincere; otherwise a line like 'I must return some video tapes', diminishes your personal brand.

10. Your restaurant choices

When attending dinner with a psychopath, it's best to let them order and book it; that way, you continue to enhance your personal brand while also staying alive, unlike this waiter if he says the wrong thing:

Waiter: Would you like to hear today's specials?

Bateman: Not if you want to keep your spleen.

Clearly, where you are seen is personal brand enhancing. It says something about you and your brand values. Being seen in a fine dining restaurant says something different to being seen in McDonald's. Context is key too: weekday versus weekend, business or family/social/partner.

However, wherever you are, your personal brand will be there for you. People will recognise you if you're doing your personal branding right. Perception of your personal brand is everything in the execution of your personal branding strategy.

Chapter Seventeen

Darth Vader's Top 10 Personal Branding Tips

One of my favourite dark characters of all time is Darth Vader. Darth Vader has been a personal favourite of mine since I saw the first *Star Wars film, A New Hope* in 1977, right up to my favourite film of 2016, *Star Wars: Rogue One*. Darth Vader has always inspired me through his personal branding. Here are my top 10 inspirational tips from Darth Vader about his personal brand enhancement strategy.

1. Black is the new black.

The first and last times that I encountered Darth Vader in *A New Hope* and *Rogue One*, he is followed by a line of white Storm Troopers as he bursts through a white spaceship door, all dressed in black, killing everything in his way.

I always remember thinking, 'Wow!' the first time, and 40+ years later I practically jumped off my seat and exclaimed, 'Wow'! I have seen *Rogue One* three times, and each time I get goosebumps during the final scene when Darth Vader leads his Storm Troopers, refusing to let anything get in his way. The total blackness, head-to-toe (no less!), makes a grand and bold statement.

Your personal brand is always enhanced with black. If you are 7 feet tall and brandishing a light sabre with the dark side of the force your ally, it makes an even bigger personal branding statement.

2. How you dress is how you're perceived.

Darth Vader isn't just wearing a normal black suit; he is wearing a black helmet mask that immediately captures your attention and an enormous black cloak that is combined with substantial black body armour. When Darth Vader walks, or rather strides purposefully, into a room, you know about it.

If Darth Vader is using the force to wipe out everything in his way, while at the same time deflecting all weapons fired at him using a light sabre that pulverises his opponents, then you certainly know that he has arrived. Never has there been a more powerful and charismatic entrance that reflects his personal brand than when Darth Vader walks through those doors.

3. Your mannerisms say everything about you.

There is nothing more distinctive in the world than Darth Vader's breathing. Everyone knows when they hear that spine-chilling sound that he is present. He doesn't even need to be seen for you to know that he is there. That is the ultimate in personal branding. People know who you are because of very distinctive personal characteristics.

4. Voice Projection

Darth Vader projects a commanding voice. He is not a man for long speeches. He is short and focused in his wording. He makes his point, turns around, and as his black cloak swooshes behind him, he is gone.

Darth Vader's voice projection is powerful and highly authoritative. You listen to what he has to say. These are excellent personal branding characteristics.

5. Red Light Sabre

Darth Vader's red light sabre is key to his personal branding while at work. The good guys have blue and white light sabres; whereas Darth

Vader (and all bad guys) have blood red, warning red, run-away red light sabres.

The personal brand is enhanced by knowing that the red light sabre spells trouble and should be avoided at all costs. It is literally a warning not to mess with him. His personal branding is enhanced by his 'work' instruments.

It's not as if I can actually imagine Darth Vader taking time out to go to the movies, attend a football match, or enjoy a nice meal. The only time you ever see him not working is when he is in a chemical bath before the black body armour goes back on. Again, an excellent work ethic is very brand enhancing.

6. The Dark Side

Any personal brand has to have a vision, a belief system, a culture, and a direction for that brand to have full effect and fulfil its potential. The Dark Side is the ethos, the creed by which Darth Vader not only lives but tries to get everyone else to follow.

The Dark Side is omnipresent, and it is everything to Darth Vader. It is the reason for his being and the reason he leads battles with such determination, purpose, and energy. The Dark Side is the part of his personal brand that is unquestionable and intrinsic to his personal brand. It dictates his actions and his motivation. Everyone needs their Dark Side to give them purpose and focus on accentuating their personal brand.

7. A Boss Who Is More Fearsome Than You

Darth Vader has the ultimate mentor, referrer, and icon to inspire his personal brand and drive his ambitions, almost like his father, The Emperor. As fearsome as Darth Vader is, nothing compares with The Emperor. The Emperor is not as impressive from a personal branding point of view or as youthful, but he is more powerful, ruthless, and nasty. The Emperor is the dark, black heart of the Dark Side.

As a role model, which we all need for our personal branding, The Emperor is as good as they come. Always giving advice and directing while always being there, Darth Vader, like anyone else, can learn a lot about personal branding from him.

8. Leadership

Darth Vader is not one of those Roman or World War 1 or 2 generals sitting in bunkers or on horses miles from the action. Darth Vader literally leads by example. The *Star Wars* films are full of him leading his Storm Troopers into battle.

Brandishing his red light sabre, striding into battle with his black cloak of danger behind him, using The Force to deflect all lasers and wipe aside anyone who will try to stop him, Darth Vader is leading by example.

In the last battle scene of *A New Hope*, it's Darth Vader who takes the lead to try to find and kill his son, Luke Skywalker. He isn't leaving this task to anyone else; it's up to him to finish the job.

From a personal branding point of view, nothing matters more to followers and employees than a leader willing to get their hands dirty and lead by example. Inspiring.

9. The Death Star

What every personal brand needs is a product: a symbol of their power and personal brand. The Death Star is Vader's. The ultimate killing force in the galaxy, the ultimate planet-erasing machine, the Death Star is that symbol of power that had been inspired by and is driven by Darth Vader.

Everyone who works for him wants to impress him with what the Death Star can do to enhance his personal brand and conquer the galaxy. Awesome.

10. Endless Optimism

I always loved the phrase that Darth Vader utters many times, 'No one can stop us this time!' Of course, his plans never quite materialise how he wishes. However, optimism and blind faith in your personal brand and ability to deliver are very intoxicating for your followers.

People follow personal brand leaders. People follow people they believe in. People would follow Darth Vader.

Chapter Eighteen

Gladiator's Top 10 Personal Branding Tips

I love *Gladiator*; it's one of my favourite films. I wanted to call my first and second sons Maximus after the general in the film, but both my first and third ex-wives (that's a blog for another day!) declined my request! So here are my top 10 favourite branding tips from *Gladiator's* Maximus:

1. Your personal brand name is your reputation.

The crux of *Gladiator* is a simple battle between good and evil. The hero is a betrayed general who is now Slave/Gladiator, Maximus Decimus. Maximus is famous for leading armies and conquering nations. His fearsome personal brand reputation goes before him.

So, Commodus, the evil emperor, tries to silence Maximus; he can't merely kill him because that way, his legend would continue. Instead, he has to try to humiliate and shatter his personal brand. Gladiator's saviour, "Manager", Proximo, says: 'You have a great name. He must kill your name before he kills you.' This is the essence of personal branding strength.

2. Your personal brand must have a vision.

My favourite line of the entire film is the spine-tingling and rousing speech that Gladiator gives after his first gladiatorial battle in front of the emperor. After killing all of the Roman army who were sent into the Coliseum to kill him and his gladiator friends, Emperor Commodus asks him his name. At first he refuses, but then he relents with one of the greatest lines of all time:

'My name is Maximus Decimus Meridius, commander of the Armies of the North, General of the Felix Legions, loyal servant to the true emperor, Marcus Aurelius, father to a murdered son, husband to a murdered wife. And I will have my vengeance, in this life or the next.'

It still makes me shudder when I read it. The gravity of that line, combined with his personal brand reputation, causes the evil emperor to pale in terror.

3. Lead by example.

The first scene of *Gladiator* is a ferocious battle between Maximus's Roman Army and the Celtic Army of savages. Maximus has a clever plan: He is going to lead his horse-backed army around the back, and while the Celts are worrying about the thousands of arrows being propelled upon them from the front, Maximus is going to lead the attack on horseback from the back to finish them off.

By leading by example, Maximus's personal brand is being enhanced. While his nemesis, Commodus, stays kilometres away in a tent, Maximus is out there murdering, maiming, and generally having a great time leading by example.

Maximus's rousing speeches inspire his cold and weary troops for one last push. His personal brand is enhanced, and people are listening to him. He will do just as he says. They will follow him.

His personal brand is so powerful that the emperor's son, Commodus (who killed his father to become emperor), fears him and consequently attempts to kill him too after this battle. Maximus, of course, gets the last word through the inspiration and loyalty he has instilled in his troops.

4. Inspire people to follow you.

Friends and people you meet just once are inspired by your personal brand too. Being able to ask or persuade or just get people to volunteer to do things for you because of who you are and what your personal brand represents is a powerful thing.

Many times in *Gladiator*, Maximus's friends, associates, and people who don't even know him are inspired by him to risk their own lives to help him. That's the ultimate in personal branding loyalty. Whether it's defending him and ultimately going to their death, or tasting his food for poison, his followers have been inspired by his personal brand to defend it in any way necessary.

Overwhelming loyalty for Maximus is also exemplified by how he can rouse and lead people that he has never met through the sheer strength of his personal brand, know-how, and experience. When he is thrust into the Coliseum to re-enact a famous battle during which he and his fellow gladiators are supposed to die, against all odds, he organises the gladiators to defeat the Roman army who was sent in to murder him.

5. Inspire enemies.

Everyone needs enemies! You need someone to measure yourself against and inspire your troops against. Hatred and fear of an enemy are just as powerful as hope and inspiration. Both are key to your personal brand.

Identifying this person or people is fundamental to how you identify your brand and your brand values. Maximus's nemesis was Emperor Commodus.

6. Live after your death.

Of course, Maximus's personal brand has a longevity to it that his nemesis, Commodus's, does not. People are inspired to carry Maximus from the Coliseum even after his death, but in contrast, loyalty towards the emperor was conspicuously lacking.

Even enemies changed sides and remembered where their loyalties were. This is the true mark of a powerful and inspiring personal brand.

7. Actions speak louder than words.

From an almost death, Maximus is coached back to life and becomes a gladiator. Not really buying the whole 'It's a show' thing, he kills people in the Coliseum as fast as possible! However, the crowd still chants his name, even though they have paid for a 3-hour show that is over in minutes because they are inspired by his personal brand. This scene ends with the memorable line: 'Are you not entertained?'

On one occasion in the Coliseum when Maximus overcame his enemies via trickery, Lucilla (one of the senators) proclaimed: 'Today I saw a slave become more powerful than the emperor of Rome'. Gladiator's personal brand had been profoundly enhanced because of his actions.

8. Be prepared for anything and go your own way.

In one of the most famous scenes from the film, Gladiator has to battle tigers and another gladiator, the King Gladiator, who is twice his size, using knowledge and skills from his personal brand.

The strength of his personal brand means that when the emperor tells him to kill the King Gladiator, Maximus defies him and lets his competitor live. His personal brand strength is further enhanced by this defiance on top of another win against all odds.

9. Never underestimate people; have empathy.

There is a very simple exchange at the beginning of Gladiator between Gladiator and one of his generals.

Quintus: People should know when they're conquered.

Maximus: Would you, Quintus? Would I?

Maximus's response demonstrates both empathy for and understanding of those fighting him, and it also shows remarkable modesty. He puts himself in their shoes and says: 'You know what? I wouldn't be conquered. That's not my personal brand and that's not our enemies' way of thinking. If I were them, I would also be fighting to the last. They are protecting and defending themselves, after all, and have nothing to lose. I would do the same'.

Understanding your competitors is key to defining your own personal brand.

10. What we do in life echoes in eternity.

Gladiator inspired his troops by reminding them that being good in battle and beyond was just as important as winning: How you win matters. Gladiator understood that your personal brand is affected by your actions now and throughout the many manifestations of your career.

Chapter Nineteen

The Godfather's Top 10 Personal Branding Tips

The Godfather is full of personal branding. Every character in it has a personal brand: some evil, some good, and in other characters, there's both good and evil. Here are my Top 10 Personal Branding Tips from *The Godfather*.

1. 'It's not what you know; it's who you know'.

The Godfather epitomises this more than anything else. It's all about your personal brand and how that engages, influences, and communicates with people, who in turn, can help you in business while reciprocally, they help you. The following quote from the film best captures this:

'Friendship is everything. Friendship is more important than talent'.

This quote communicates what everyone knows when they think about it. You can be the most talented person in the world at what you do, but without a personal brand that people respect and want to be connected with, with no network, no friends, nor associates, then your talent is meaningless.

Friends (and in this context I'm also using the word 'friends' for business associates) are the people who can make your dreams happen, and you theirs. It's quid pro quo. It's all about your personal network and your personal brand.

2. 'Someday, and that day may never come, I will call upon you to do a service for me. But until that day, accept this justice as a gift on my daughter's wedding day'.

I have a t-shirt with this slogan because it's a wonderful quote from the movie. Your personal brand is so powerful that someone comes to you for help. It is clear within the relationship that this person needs your help because you can make things happen that they cannot.

In return, you, who are helping this person, will not necessarily ask for anything in return. However, you maintain the right to do so in the event you need a favour. This is the essence of power, and a strong and awe-inspiring personal brand.

3. 'I'll make him an offer that he can't refuse'.

Clearly, there are ways of doing this, and in business, it's all about the strength and power of your personal brand, what you can use to negotiate with, and what you can offer. If you hold all the cards, then you have the best negotiating position.

You can certainly make an offer that someone cannot refuse in any context, and it's often about how far you are willing to go to achieve this that counts. How you use this power, how you get what you want, and any repercussions on your personal brand of using that power are up to you to decide.

4. 'Great men are not born great. They grow great'.

It's so true. Leaders with silver spoons in their mouths rarely become great actual leaders in the real world. You just have to look at royal families and rich dynasties across the world to see how this manifests itself.

True leaders with great personal brands are made and grown over time, and after experience. *The Godfather* is full of wannabe leaders. Not all have the charisma, nous, personal network, human touch, ruthlessness, and wisdom to make it happen.

You grow into a leader through enhancing your personal brand, adding experience, making connections, building and investing in your network, taking time to build relationships, launching and building companies, succeeding, failing, and succeeding again: These things constitute everything an entrepreneur has to endure to enhance their personal brand.

How you act with greater seniority, experience, and connections determines your personal brand's greatness.

5. 'Never hate your enemies. It affects your judgement'.

This is a great quote; it's a quote that I wish I could put into practice more often! Emotion clouds your judgement. It makes you do things that you reflect on later and wish you hadn't. Taking time to consider your response, your email reply, text reply, and other actions, can save you thousands of dollars, and it can also save harm and hurt to both yourself and others.

Business is an emotional practice. Entrepreneurs are passionate about what they do and how they do it. They are passionate about protecting their workforce, personal brand, livelihood, and shareholders from attack. How your personal brand copes, deals with, and leads through these times can determine how great an entrepreneurial leader you really are.

I use cycling and the gym to force myself to do this. If something bad happens at work, or I receive an email/text that stirs my emotions, I try to force myself to cycle/go to the gym and take time to consider a response.

These places mean that I am away from my laptop/mobile, so that I cannot respond. I also am removed from the heat of the battle in the office/out with friends/having a drink, and, therefore, cannot reply/respond.

If you combine both hatred or vengeance and alcohol together, the ramifications can be even more dangerous and everlasting. It is best to remove yourself from the situation before responding, and it is often useful to speak with neutral people, business coaches, non-executives, or friends about the situation before replying.

Your personal brand can be harmed or enhanced by thinking before acting. Acting without emotion and hatred in a cold, focused way is essential.

'It's not personal; it's business' is key to a building a powerful personal brand, and it's also a great quote from *The Godfather*.

6. 'Revenge is a dish that tastes best when served cold'.

Business is full of ups and downs, sleights, mishaps, deals that didn't turn out as you both had planned, people who let you down, or people who attempt to sabotage either you or your business. How you respond to these situations determines the strength of your personal brand, and it will also heavily influence how seriously people take you.

Act in haste and in vengeance, and you will often pay the price. Think carefully about your revenge and create a strategy to exact cold-hearted revenge; your personal brand will not only be enhanced, but your revenge will probably be more effective. The culprit will think twice before acting against you in the future and will warn others against acting against you.

It takes a great personal brand and great patience that enable you to ponder the long game: The more detailed your long-term strategy, the bigger the picture, the greater the likelihood you have of being able to rise above the desire for speed of vengeance. You want to exact your longer-term plans now, not in the future. Take your time and the satisfaction will be greater and longer lasting because you will have thought through all the angles, options, downsides, and repercussions. Your personal brand will grow in strength.

7. 'A friend should always underestimate your virtues. An enemy overestimate your faults'.

Your personal brand is multifaceted and reveals different characters to different people at different times. As this quote from *The Godfather* demonstrates, a friend should always be surprised and delighted about what you can and want to do for them.

An enemy should always think that they can get the better of you. Constantly surprising your enemies with moves and actions that they do not expect is often key to your success. Bettering your enemies in deals and life will enhance your personal brand.

8. 'The lawyer with the briefcase can steal more money than a man with a gun'.

Bearing in the mind the context of *The Godfather*, this is a great quote and captures the heart of an effective personal brand. Violence rarely achieves anything. Business is all about outsmarting your competition, working with your partners, and impressing and delivering for your clients.

Being smart in business and creating and cultivating clever and effective win-win deals will always pay off far more than acts of violence that cannot be controlled and never lead to good outcomes.

9. 'Keep your friends close and your enemies closer'.

Often in business it pays to get close to your enemies, competition, and people who want to exact vengeance against you or get the better of you. You can find out more about them close-by, determine how they work, find out what they're up to, and discover what they're planning. That way, you can win their confidence and then take action when they least expect it.

Your personal brand is seen in many ways by friends and enemies. Keeping people unaware of your real intentions, or as this quote says, keeping you enemies closer than your friends, sounds cynical, but it is very pragmatic advice in the long term. It also accentuates your personal brand.

10. 'Time erodes gratitude more than it does beauty'.

I love this quote from *The Godfather*. It makes me think that for your personal brand to thrive, survive, and become even more powerful and effective, you really need to invest in your relationships, build you network, and keep maintaining these networks. People forget easily.

Never take anything for granted, always reach out to people, be proactive, and don't always leave it to other people to do this. If they don't and you don't, you both lose out. You also soon find out who your trustworthy and reliable friends and business associates are, so that you can help each other.

People forget. Remind them. Your personal brand grows increasingly strong as you do so.

Chapter Twenty

Using Your Personal Branding to Develop a Portfolio Career

When reading about my career, it is important to realise that much of the work I do now and the main strands of my portfolio career based around LinkedIn would have been neither possible nor even existed before 2003.

In my career, I have demonstrated that when you embrace the entrepreneurial spirit, it is possible to reinvent yourself, create a business from scratch, and turn it into something quite different, yet special. The fact that I talk about 'passion portfolios' says it all.

I am the founder and global CEO of Black Marketing, a global marketing consultancy that specialises in enabling LinkedIn for C-suite executives and entrepreneurs across the world. I have taken the company from one person in one country in 2014 to a full listing on NASDAQ in 2016.

I have other claims to fame, most notably as the only NASDAQ-listed CEO with a Mohawk hairstyle. I have also been named as an Official LinkedIn Power Profile every year between 2012 and 2017, and I have one of the world's most viewed LinkedIn profiles with over 55,000 followers. My profile is ranked #1 in Singapore, I have hundreds of recommendations, I am one of the top 100 most influential LinkedIn Bloggers, and I am a #1 international best- selling author with my book, *LinkedIn Mastery for Entrepreneurs*.

My late grandfather always told me that success depends on who you know rather than what you know, and LinkedIn has proved him right. I am also an experienced event speaker and chairperson for conferences, company events, and I regularly hold LinkedIn workshops.

I write passionately about all aspects of marketing and business for various media brands. I have also been featured in various books, and I am heavily involved with the Singapore Management University Mentorship programme for final-year marketing students at SMU's Business School. This is an unpaid, voluntary part of my portfolio that I really value to help inspire and develop future entrepreneurs.

What made me decide to leave the UK and move away from my previous business career?

A mixture of reasons really. One of them was the fact I was an entrepreneur in the UK who wanted to be an entrepreneur in Asia. I wanted to test myself over here and have more flexibility, but also more empowerment in terms of working for myself. However, there was also a catalyst: two previous employers who didn't pay me! I had to basically sue them to get the money I was rightly owed. I also didn't want to be in the position where I was relying on somebody else to pay me ever again, especially in a different region, such as Asia.

This meant I had more control over who paid me, who I worked for, and what I did. Taking back control also meant I could actually build a business of my own, as opposed to making money for other people, and it also gave me the flexibility to express my passions for other things.

I now have the flexibility to work how I want. Today I am in Hong Kong, next week I will be in Manilla, the week after I will be in Shanghai, and then I will be back home to Singapore. So, I have the flexibility to move around because it's my business. I also want to develop it how I want to, and I couldn't do that if I worked for somebody else. You'd have to get approval for this and approval for that. But having a passion for the business and owning it yourself, there's nothing quite like it.

In the Business of Connecting

When I first came to Singapore, I knew no one. Therefore, I reached out on LinkedIn to ask people to introduce me to people they knew in Singapore. They did. I got my first, second, and third jobs in Singapore through connecting with people on LinkedIn.

None of these jobs actually existed or were advertised before I connected with and met the people in charge. They were created for me because, having met me, they thought I fit the vision of where the business was going, and my skills, personality, and experience inspired them to create the job for me. It all happened through networking.

All of these roles were regional roles, which meant that I started using LinkedIn, even more, to find the right people in Asia Pacific to connect with, message, and talk to. China, India, Japan, Australia, Kuala Lumpur, Jakarta, you name it. I could find a chief marketing officer (CMO) of a brand in that country using LinkedIn. By using LinkedIn, I was also able to find decision-makers, chief executives, CMOs, people who had budgets, and I won them as clients. LinkedIn enabled me to build a pipeline that I could not have done any other way across Asia Pacific.

I quickly realised that aside from reaching out to people on LinkedIn to find key connections, you could also use LinkedIn to win business and find jobs as well.

So, I started doing training, and I started getting asked to do training in LinkedIn across the world. Then, people started asking to pay me for managing their LinkedIn accounts. I saw there was a business opportunity here in Singapore, the same way as when I was an entrepreneur in the UK. I could live my passion for connecting myself and other people socially to help senior executives and entrepreneurs also connect when they didn't have the time, experience, or the expertise to do it themselves. Hence, my Black Marketing company was formed.

How did I develop my portfolio career?

I started developing a portfolio career. It basically came out of people contacting me saying, 'I want to work with you; I can see your talents,

I can see your experience, I can see your contacts, but I can't afford your rates'. So, I thought there's got to be another way of doing this. I'll create a company that basically controls stakes in companies or has stakes in companies.

We don't take cash payments; we take share payments, so we get paid in shares. Therefore, we have a stake in the company. If the company does well, and it uses our Black Marketing LinkedIn services, then we do well because we could then sell our stake and we can make more money than by just getting fees. If we don't do very well for them, they have the option to buy back our stake at competitive or nominal rates.

Essentially, I'm taking a gamble based on my experience and my faith in my Black Marketing company's ability to drive business for other people because we're not getting paid. So, therefore, it is really a passion. It's not something we sweat equity for. You could call it a 'passion equity' if such a term exists. Thereby, I'm saying I believe in you as a person and a business.

You just need some help in terms of your LinkedIn. Therefore, I'll help you, but in return, you're giving me a stake of your business. We have a wide range of businesses where we have stakes that I wouldn't otherwise be involved in. They range from content marketing, social media marketing, digital marketing, to wine, yoga, management consulting, and leadership training. I'm very open to the idea because of the fact I have a real passion for helping other entrepreneurs.

Another real passion of mine is speaking. These requests are also coming mainly from Asia.

People didn't really know how to use LinkedIn, so they turned to me and asked, 'How do you use LinkedIn? Can you do a talk about it?' And that turned into 'Can you do a workshop?' And that turned into 'Can you come to Kuala Lumpur, Jakarta, Bangkok, Sydney, Shanghai, Guangzhou, or Hong Kong to present?'

This is fantastic. I get to talk about my passion, I get to travel the world, meet some great people, and they'll pay me at the same time! And it helps my LinkedIn business too. What more could I ask?

What is my main business income stream?

This is definitely Black Marketing. I started Black Marketing a couple of years ago in Singapore with one person, and now it's global. So, that's the real premium breadwinner: dealing with C-Suite executives and getting paid to develop their LinkedIn profiles, their personal profiles, their company profiles, their personal brand, their company brand, their content marketing strategy, and win them new business. That is really the key to success in all the other ventures because it helps fund all the other ventures. So, if Black Marketing wasn't doing very well, I couldn't afford to have the other passion portfolios.

What do I do in the way of voluntary work in my passion portfolio?

The voluntary stuff is with the chambers. So, I do a lot for both the American Chamber of Commerce in Singapore and the British Chamber of Commerce in Singapore, and I am on a number of committees. What I love about this work is we're putting on events for the members and seeking out speakers who are experts in their field. We don't get paid for it: We do it for the profile, we do it for the engagement. We also do it as we have a passion for hearing what other people have to say, and a passion for really listening and learning from experts in various fields.

On the British Chamber, I'm in the ICT committee, the entrepreneur committee, and the marketing committee. Therefore, this covers my three passion areas, which is amazing! I help the chamber build, help the British and the American companies build in Singapore, and basically help the members learn a lot more things. This also involves another passion, networking, which is fantastic because you meet so many interesting people. Essentially, getting involved in these chambers is kind of like a labour of love.

I'm also a mentor for SMU, which is Singapore Management University's final-year graduates, and I open that up for other people, and other marketing graduates as well. I do various speeches too at different universities. I often get people coming up to me afterwards asking if I will mentor them. Of course, it's a pleasure to do so, as long as they're not working for Microsoft, Google, or something like that. It's really good because you're giving something back as well. You also get to see them grow, and they'll always remember you helped them grow. So, when they become chairman or chief executive of Google, I hope they will still remember me and what I have done for them!

Ex-Pat Life in Singapore

It's very easy being an ex-pat in Singapore. It's much easier in Singapore than places like Hong Kong or Shanghai because it's English-speaking first. In Hong Kong, it is very difficult to even communicate with taxi drivers. Singapore is very much a Western society, with around a third of the population not Singaporean, but ex-pats of some kind. It's also a multicultural, multi-racial society, which gives equal weight to all religions and races, and it has policies to make sure there's no friction.

You're always going to get some people complaining about ex-pats being over here to steal local jobs, but that's rarely the case. All the jobs I've created as a business owner didn't exist before, so I think ex-pats are equally as important as Singaporeans. There is a plethora of rules and regulations in terms of who can apply for jobs and how many Singaporeans you are obligated to employ.

However, with unemployment around 1%, there's full employment here, so people can pick and choose. Accordingly, it's a great place to work, and it is also great because it's very much a hub of Asia. It's very much the place people use as a regional base, so it's wonderful to be an ex-pat here.

Would I ever go back to a typical one company employed role?

No, never in a million years. Never! I'd rather work for myself and fail than work for somebody else and succeed. Because even succeeding with somebody else does not give you the same satisfaction as trying to work for yourself. Even if things don't work for you, you learn so many lessons. You just make sure you don't make those mistakes the next time, and then you can build a business as a result.

I've been an entrepreneur for over 20 years, on and off, and it's fantastic, especially in Asia. Therefore, I am never going back to work for somebody else. Working for yourself enables you to be more positive and actually work for who you want to, when you want to, and have more control. You can travel when you want to, and you can do what you want—just as long as you have the business fundamentals and foundation in place. It's important to have good people around you.

Why 'passion, pleasure, and profit' in that order?

I firmly believe that you have to be passionate about what you do. The most miserable people you ever meet are people who make a lot of money but aren't very passionate about what they do. So, you have to be passionate about what you do. I'm very lucky in that I've worked in the music industry, TV, and radio as well. I'm very passionate about music, and I've worked in sports and for the Internet and various different industry newspapers and magazines, where I was absolutely passionate about the work I did.

Having a passion for something is brilliant. However, combine it with being your passion and building it because you're passionate about the business, and it is even better. I get a lot of pleasure from doing LinkedIn myself. I get pleasure from doing it for other people. I get pleasure in combining LinkedIn with building up somebody else's business and getting paid for it, which enables me to make a profit.

If I turned that around and I asked, 'How am I going to make a profit first?' I might as well just go into banking or financial services because you're not getting a lot of enjoyment. You've got a lot of stress, and that's not what I ever want. I always want to be passionate and never think about work as being work; that's the key to being an entrepreneur.

I think you always look at your pleasure and your passion and your work as the same thing. It's not a chore to do the work. You don't mind doing it on Saturdays, you don't mind doing it on Sundays. You don't mind getting involved and getting stuck in and rolling up your sleeves and working late if you have to, and networking, because you're building a business. And that's really because it's pleasurable.

I love meeting new people and developing businesses for them. I can't imagine just going out there and thinking, 'OK, I need to make money, I need to make money', because that is not very pleasurable. It's also very stressful because you're putting an undue burden on yourself. Whereas, if you work for your passions, the profit will come. Because you're so committed and you're so passionate about what you do, the profit comes along automatically, providing your business model is right, your service model is right, and your fundamentals are right.

What does success mean for me?

In summary, I would say it goes back to what my granddad said, 'It's not what you know, it's who you know'. Having a 'passion portfolio', you work with people you want to, you help people you really want to. You get a lot of pleasure from working with people you like, doing work you like, and getting a lot of advocates. That's really the key. Life's very short, and if you can also help other people build their businesses at the same time, then that's fantastic. It's win-win!

Key Learning Points from Chris's Story

With the right mindset, belief, and positive action, it is possible to reinvent yourself and create a new business and 'passion portfolio' in a completely different country and culture.

Singapore is a country that embraces entrepreneurial spirit, but do your 'homework' first.

The power of LinkedIn cannot be underestimated—it's your main shop window to the world to develop and optimise your networks, and also to open up and create new work opportunities.

By becoming an expert you can create income streams by sharing your knowledge to help benefit other people, and there are always spin-off benefits to other aspects of your portfolio.

Inspirational and motivational specialist speakers are always in demand, and it's even better if you can travel the world and get paid for sharing your passion.

Any voluntary aspect of your portfolio can also add kudos to your brand and reputation.

If your passions feature as strands of business, and you are also passionate about developing your business, you have the ideal winning combination.

Success is not what you know; it's who you know!

Chapter Twenty-One

How Prince, David Beckham, and Gareth Emery All Used Personal Branding to Develop Their Businesses

Prince: A Personal Brand That Was Truly Gold

People are always shocked when rockstars die early, but given their lives and the way that they work, people really shouldn't be surprised. They should appreciate the artist's material while they can. The great thing about rockstars is that their music lives on. Prince died due to a very rock-star reason—a suspected overdose—but his personal brand and his music will live on.

Being a rock and pop fan who loved music in the 1980s, I grew up with Prince. Later, I was lucky enough to see him on his Purple Rain and Symbol tours, and I loved the album, *Purple Rain* (1999), but less so his other 47 albums. I always admired how he kept his personal brand and content marketing. It did not always appeal to me personally, but I always admired his experimentation and creativity.

The ingenuity of his performances was exemplified at the Super Bowl when he played during a thunder and lightening storm; he didn't care about his safety or about promoting his current material. He just played songs that people knew, and he put on a show for the global audience. That's what his personal presence was all about: spine-tingling performance, and at the end of a medley, he played "Purple Rain" in the pouring rain. You couldn't script it: It hadn't rained at a Super Bowl before this night.

Prince was way ahead of his time in terms of understanding that to remain successful in the public eye, you have to change your own brand and your content marketing strategy (in his case, his music, videos, film, books, live tours, etc.) every year. He certainly did that. He knew to keep his fans and his customers as advocates: He had to be constantly changing, keeping it fresh, and being ahead of the game.

His first hits happened in the 1970s, and his last was in 2016. He truly transformed himself as the decades of pop, fashion, and music tastes changed. Not everything he did was successful. In fact, you could argue that having launched so many different versions of his personal brand and so many albums, most of the things he did were not successful. Yet, his personal brand overcame and superseded all barriers; that was its strength. People admired his creative diversity.

Prince released an enormous 50 albums during his career, which is a phenomenal number. Unfortunately, only some of them were great. Some of these albums he generated just to get out of his record contracts, which he always felt constricted him. He wasn't afraid of failure, and he wasn't afraid to try different angles, different techniques, and different sounds, even if they alienated the more mainstream fans.

Prince's purple patch was definitely his early years of 'Purple Rain', '1999', 'Sign o' the Times' with 'Diamonds and Pearls' while he was Prince, and before he became the symbol of New Power Generation.

The change in his name, which became known as The Artist Formerly Known as Prince, or just Symbol or Love Symbol, hindered the promoters who wanted to market his live shows. I remember my radio group in the UK were co-promoting his UK tour and were not allowed under any circumstances to call him Prince. We had to market the shows by citing the name, plus Symbol. Eventually they let us say, The Artist Formerly Known as Prince. It was just bizarre!

However, Prince (Symbol at the time) also made it very clear that he was no longer going to be playing any of his Prince stuff and would only play Symbol music (his new album). This made marketing and selling his shows a nightmare to say the least.

It did, though, generate millions of dollars of free PR (not all good), but for pop stars, all PR is good PR! The tickets did not sell out, but it did create interest.

Ironically, Symbol then became known as The Artist Formerly Known as Prince, which bordered on the ridiculous. However, the tabloids lapped it up. That and his many creative fashion statements, lovers, and cameo appearances in film, TV, and on albums (some known, others anonymous) all propelled his brand, accentuated it, and kept it fresh and interesting.

The change in his name did seem to tie in with his music becoming less consumer-friendly and with fewer sales. Prince blamed social media, YouTube, and iTunes for this. He is still not on Spotify. It's very hard to find any official videos of his on YouTube for this reason.

Prince's brand values shone through all his personas and material. He was always original, creative, unexpected, experimental, diverse, never trying to please all the people all of the time, charismatic, and at times he was egotistical while at other times he was anonymous. Above all, he was about his music and what it meant to his fans, old and new, who appreciated it. He must have been one of the hardest-working pop stars in the world, constantly creating and performing on his albums and other people's, his shows and other people's.

'All that glitters ain't gold' is a lyric from his 'Gold' song, and there could not be a better way of summing him up. Not everything he did was amazing, but his personal brand was dynamic and shone through everything amazingly. It always glittered like gold, despite everything. Now it always will.

Gareth Emery—A Really Personal Brand

When I see a great underrated brand, I love to highlight it. When I see someone doing something and going against the grain, I also like to highlight it. Trance star, Gareth Emery, brings me so much personal pleasure through his inspiring, touching, and energetic songs, so I wanted to highlight him and his new album, and how he uses content to market his personal brand through social media, talk about the inspiration behind his new album, *100 Reasons to Live*, and discuss why it has led him to switch off his phone and his social media.

In 2015, I wrote about the amazing Armin Van Buuren, A State of Trance. Gareth Emery doesn't have the same PR, clout, or kudos as Van Buuren, but to me, he produces as many if not more truly great trance anthems that make the hairs on the back of your neck stand up. I love working to trance, and I love cycling to trance. It makes me go faster at both!

The way Emery has packaged his content has always been interesting too. Trance artists have many vehicles to express themselves: studio albums, singles, mix albums, tours, etc.

Emery started with podcasts and grew that into his current Electric for Life content brand, which combines a weekly radio show with online and offline content, album releases, etc. He has really understood the power of content and how to express and communicate it under one brand.

Of course, Emery uses all the usual social platforms and has a decent following on each:

Spotify: 907,640 monthly followers

YouTube: 146,000, but his most viewed video has gained over 5 million views and is his best, most haunting song (in my opinion)

SoundCloud: 129,000 followers

Twitter: 573,000 followers

FaceBook: 1.4 million followers

Instagram: 154,000 followers

LinkedIn: Well, he's not perfect: Neither he nor his company is on LinkedIn.

The difference to me between Emery and the other trance DJs is the way he combines uplifting trance music with an evocative, female vocalist who often sings about much darker things from death to heartbreak. The combination is irresistible and leads to some of those most memorable and emotional songs produced from the the trance genre of music.

'Concrete Angel', 'U', 'Going Home', 'Hands', 'Dynamite', 'Soldier', 'Long Way from Home', the latest single, 'Reckless', and many more, all fall into this category.

He even shows how talented he is with the piano in an acoustic version of his new song, 'Save Me', which is worth listening to.

With the new album, Gareth Emery has reached deep into the personal psyche and revealed his inner unhappiness at being a millionaire music star, and expressed how he realised that he wasn't appreciating the things that matter despite having all the money and possessions he could want.

Emery is rare in that having all the material comforts has not made him happier, and as a result, he switches his phone off, doesn't go on social media, so that he can experience and appreciate his personal life. In the competitive world of trance music, that takes guts, and even more so to actually reveal it publicly.

In an interesting interview with *Your EDM*, he talks about fearing that he was a one-hit wonder and having no bookings at all back in 2006. From despair like this (as any entrepreneur will tell you) comes two things: 1) you give up and go do something else; 2) you start working harder than ever to show that you are not a one-hit wonder. He did the latter and turned it around. How many businesses and how many entrepreneurs choose the former and never fulfil their potential?

Emery's personal brand is real and visceral: In a FaceBook post, which he used to launch his new album, he explained the title and ethos behind it:

'Strange but true fact: about two years ago, I was so miserable.

I didn't have any reason to be. I was reasonably successful, in a job that I loved, was married to a beautiful wife, lived in an amazing house, had no recent major tragedy in my life, or any of the other things that make people unhappy, yet I was pretty much constantly annoyed.

Why? Because a festival I wanted to play at wouldn't book me. Because I wanted to stay in a suite, but the promoter would only book me a standard room. Because my brand-new Lamborghini was going to take nine months to be delivered from the factory, when I wanted it in six.

You probably hate me reading that. I don't blame you. Reading this back, I hate me too.

However, there is a depressing trend that I have noticed amongst famous and successful DJs: just how many of them are really unhappy. They're travelling the world, living a lifelong dream that took decades of work to accomplish, and yet they're constantly upset because they were given Moet instead of Cristal, or because one person on social media said they hated their new record. Boohoo. Bring out the violins.

That was how 100 Reasons to Live got its name.

I saw myself turning into an archetypal miserable DJ and decided that was not the person I wanted to be.

I figured out that happiness and a love of life doesn't come from career success or material wealth; in fact, some of the happiest people I knew were, on paper, some of the less successful.

Now, I'm not saying 'don't make money' or 'don't be successful'. I happen to be a fan of both. But I learned that those things alone don't make me happy.

What does make me happy? Many things. Sunshine. Walking outside. Beers at the pub with friends. Taking my daughter to music class. Lazy Sundays. Sunsets. Swimming.

Turning off my phone, logging out of emails, getting off the social media hamster wheel, and engaging the world around me—something which I'd totally lost the ability to do.

In short, I rediscovered what made me happy, or in other words, figured out my Reasons To Live'.

Inspiring. How many of us can claim to have this work/life balance sorted out to this extent? Switching off the world, turning off social media, letting go of the phone . . . the thought probably sends shivers down your back. Of course, he's right, but it's easier to say than do.

Brand Beckham Is the Ultimate Personal Brand

According to a new *Forbes* study, David Beckham has been in the news in recent years for being the 2nd most lucrative retired sports star behind Michael Jordan. This is quite an amazing achievement for an English footballer, or as he is now known, fashion/advertising icon. Beckham is a great example of how developing a personal brand pays off, literally forever.

Arnold Palmer made $1.8 million in winnings during his PGA career. He earned 22 times that in 2015, thanks to the strength of the Palmer brand. Michael Jordan banked more than $4 million in salary only twice during his 15 NBA seasons. This year he'll receive more than any other athlete on the planet, retired or active. That's the power of personal branding.

(In the old days, he would take anyone willing to pay . . .)

In a recent edition of *GQ*, there were no less than three advertisements featuring David Beckham. I can remember none of the brands: Two were clothing and one was perfume, but I do remember Brand Beckham.

Beckham, and his very savvy wife, Victoria (aka Posh Spice), have performed an amazing marketing exercise in creating such an inspirational, holistic Beckham brand. They have ensured that brands from every sector wish to be associated with them. Well, actually him.

David Beckham out-shines his wife in the association and financial stakes by a significant margin. But don't rule her out as one of the clever advisers behind the scenes; she has a great understanding of marketing and a profound grasp of the power of the personality brand on the contemporary public.

However, I think there is also a risk of overexposure for the Beckham brand at the expense of all the brands they endorse. The effect of this is that consumers remember none of the brands that Beckham is endorsing and just remember him.

That is, of course, great news for the David Beckham brand, and with every increase in exposure, it no doubt helps persuade other brands to pay ever-increasing amounts of money to be associated with him. I have to question the value that they are receiving though.

Three advertisements in GQ all feature Beckham looking decidedly moody, and the brands he is promoting just get lost. Repetition of one brand (i.e., the Beckham brand) over single advertisements for the others is bound to promote him and not them. What value are the brands themselves getting out of this relationship?

Beckham has a global sponsorship with the Sands Group who own the iconic Marina Bay Sands (MBS) in Singapore. Every time he visits, there is a media circus, which creates great buzz. He even walks on water . . .

I do find it odd that Beckham is the iconic face of a casino or 'integrated resort' as we call it here. (In Singapore we call MBS an integrated resort as we pretend we don't have two casinos that make as much money as the whole of Las Vegas put together. Fifteen percent of the gross revenue of both go straight to the people of Singapore via the government, but I digress) Why him? What are the brand values of Beckham that match MBS?

MBS is a casino with luxury retail, filled with restaurants and bars of all kinds and all levels, including my favourite in Singapore, DB Modern Bistro & Oyster Bar. Occupancy is 100% every night for the 3,000 rooms, so where does Beckham fit in?

Does he have any brand values that match MBS or, in fact, to Asia? To me, no. But this is a classic case of relationships in LA and clever brand positioning of Beckham by his management and wife (the power behind the pretty face). It's personal brand personified: powerful, but without reason.

I am, therefore, not sure that there is even a strategy as to what kind of brands Beckham goes for. Diageo announced that they were recruiting Beckham to be their Haig Club Whiskey brand. Strangely, they are using Beckham to emphasise the heritage of the product and its preeminence, rather than Sean Connery, Kevin Spacey, or Christopher Lee.

I would never have associated heritage and history with Beckham, so to me, it's an odd choice. Clearly, Diageo did their research, and he's an inspirational icon to the target audience, who are presumably much younger than other whiskey brands—more Johnnie Walker and F1 than Famous Grouse and Teachers.

The brands Beckham is associated with are eclectic, to the say the least. As well as Diageo, he has worked for or is currently working for Pepsi, Police Sunglasses, Sainsbury's (in the UK), Young's Frozen Fish, H&M, Armani, Belstaff, Adidas, Brietling for Bentley, Burger King,

Walt Disney, Diet Coke, Samsung, and the list goes on; plus, there are his own brands of perfume, games, as well as a clothing line.

Beckham also has a 5-year pact with British fashion brand Kent & Curwen, which is worth $8 million USD annually, plus royalties for the collection that was launched in the second half of 2016. Although this again is more about relationships, it does at least have something to do with sport because it will see the former English captain design ranges and promote the brand overseas.

The deal is the first to come out of Beckham and his business partner, Simon Fuller's joint venture with Hong Kong-listed Global Brands Group last year, called Seven Global. Kent & Curwen's parent company, Trinity, is owned by the same family that set up Global Brands.

Another odd partnership is with the Chinese real estate firm, Luneng, who inked the British footballer to a pact worth more than $5 million USD per year to be a vague 'ambassador'. The explanation as to this partnership is vague and odd, to say the least: 'David Beckham is a great fit with Luneng Group's developmental strategy because of his positivity and high sense of social responsibility'. Luneng hopes to demonstrate its ecological lifestyle's fit through the partnership even though Luneng's portfolio includes the integrated development of coal alongside renewable energy and real estate. So, Beckham is a front person for the least ecologically friendly energy source on the planet, coal. Pretty face to conceal a hard business?

A more logical sponsorship is with Sky TV in the UK as they battle BT for viewers of the English Premier League that they share the rights to. His personal brand comes across extremely well, of course, and with his background in football, clearly, this makes so much sense from a brand values point of view.

Of course, the advertisement does as much to promote the personal brand of David Beckham as it does to promote Sky.

From David Beckham's point of view, why would you turn down the millions being offered if brands are daft enough to think that they will cut through where many others have previously failed? It is more likely that any associated brand will have gained a short-term spike with the launch PR.

It is noticeable that of all the brands that he is involved with, not many continue a relationship after the initial term, perhaps because their brand tracking is showing that he is associated with too many brands, and, therefore, there is less to be gained from the association.

In my view, there is little chance of any long-term brand building by the association, but many brand owners will gladly hitch a ride to the Beckham brand building machine for a short-term hit. They must have it now. Ironically, all these brand associations may leave the individual brands behind, but they keep building brand Beckham to greater heights and are very much part of the Beckham personal branding strategy.

David Beckham could learn a lot from Shaquille O'Neal, who is on LinkedIn. Beckham has no profile; whereas Shaquille does have a cool one, captioned, 'Conveyor of Fun'.

PS: He doesn't really walk on water . . .

Chapter Twenty-Two

Who Has the Greatest Personal Brand, Musk, Gates, or Jobs?

I read an excellent biography earlier this year on Elon Musk, by Ashlee Vance titled *Tesla, Space X and the Quest for a Fantastic Future*, which as an entrepreneur, is absolutely inspiring! The book I read before that was *Steve Jobs*, the biography by Walter Isaacson. I am yet to source Bill Gates's biography to complete my reading of the dynamic trio.

Reading Vance's book about Musk got me thinking when he posed the question: Who is the greatest technology entrepreneur among Gates, Jobs, and Musk? He believes that Musk is superior because he has achieved so much in so many different areas, and he still has half his life to lead. I decided to compile pros and cons for each of the three. What do you think? Who is the greatest?

Steve Jobs

Pros:
Jobs was a self-made billionaire, an adopted child by a poor family that was able to get together just enough money to send him to college and start his business venture/education. Jobs created the world's most valuable company in Apple (it just slipped into 2nd behind Alphabet/ Google), and Jobs created the world's most profitable company in Apple. Moreover, Jobs created the Apple brand with an emotional attachment to it. He dramatised Apple's stores, he maintained a charismatic figure

with his new product presentations, storytelling, and natural ability to convince customers that by acquiring a mass market product, you can 'think different'.

Jobs was creative and his sense of design was inspired by studying areas that were unrelated to his business and background, including observing the world around him, calligraphy, and travelling to India. Jobs had the ability to say no and stay focused, and when he came back to Apple in 1997, there were 350 products in Apple's catalogue, which he reduced to just 10.

Simplicity was key to him. Jobs worked with passion: 'Choose a career you love and you will never have to work a day in your life' from Confucius was his motto.

Always knowing his own value and worth, he never flaunted his money. Jobs has always been very intuitive and was very good at predicting the market, using his intuition, analysing trends, and pondering questions, like 'How would a child use a phone/tablet?' The touchscreen concept created immense product innovation, including, The Apple II, the Mac, the iPod, the iPhone, and the iPad. Jobs changed the music industry forever through digital downloads, iTunes, and the iPod, and he accomplished what no one within the industry could do or would dare to even attempt.

Jobs changed the film industry through Pixar to such an extent that Disney bought it for 5 billion USD, which is a phenomenal amount of money for a small studio that produces only one film per year. Although he created NeXt, which was a disaster, it did include one or two aspects that the old Apple needed, and this then propelled them to buy NeXt.

He created value from something that failed—a remarkable talent. Jobs had the ability to recognise his only weaknesses; he couldn't engineer or design, so he brought in people who could while he could organise, visualise, lead, and evangelise these talents to remarkable levels. Jobs did not let money change him, and he remained modest throughout his career at Apple. He loved creating a buzz and excitement surrounding his products; he was genuinely excited and believed in what he was creating

Cons:

At a personal level, he was a terrible father who denied the paternity of his daughter, Lisa, for many years until just before his death. He called the first Apple computer, Lisa, presumably after the daughter he denied having. If you watch the film titled *Steve Jobs,* it actually spends more time on this issue in his life than anything else.

Jobs lost his temper with employees for small mistakes and created an infamous, toxic, and oppressive workplace, with as many people hating him as adoring him. Many people believe that Steve Wozniak was the true genius behind Apple, with Jobs merely being the highly visible front man, and the sales guy who turned a concept into a brand.

Jobs was no engineer, nor was he a designer. He created NeXT, which failed, but NeXT was, nevertheless, used later in some of the Macs. Jobs only donated to charity once. Greenpeace and other environmental groups targeted Jobs over his company's lack of ecological credentials, claiming that the company showed little dedication to reducing waste or recycling. Jobs cared little for pay and conditions of his workers in factories in China and Asia where parts of the Apple products were created. Jobs was the first one to leave the battlefield.

Bill Gates

Pros:

Gates is a hands-on guy: He wrote the code himself for BASIC and kept coding 5 years after Microsoft was invented. Gates created what was the world's most valuable company, and the company remains one of the world's most valuable and profitable companies. Gates invented the market of the software business: Microsoft was the first company that created revenue, and he made Windows, which is the default operating system in the world.

Gates is the number one humanitarian on the planet. In 1975, a 19-year-old Bill Gates read an article about the Altair 8800, a new microcomputer. He contacted the computer's manufacturer to say that he and his friends were creating an interface to allow the computer language BASIC to run on the Altair.

He didn't let the fact that he didn't have an Altair and could, therefore, not write code for one, slow him down. Gates started off being fantastically innovative and creative with the Office suite of products concept, ubiquitous on every PC in the world, as the default business software.

Cons:

Gates focused on rapid expansion and less on creativity and customer satisfaction. Microsoft reached its all-time peak in market capitalisation in September of 2000, when the stock was worth $642 billion. Today, it is worth only about a third as much at $290 billion, which is 40% less than Apple. Gates had no problems in violating corporate law to kill competition, and he benefits from maintaining a monopoly.

Gates tried to prevent open-source software, like Linux, to develop. Gates could have done what Jobs did but stopped innovating to focus on humanitarian issues when he realised that he could no longer innovate to the extent that he had originally done nor in the same way that Jobs did. In fact, Gates could significantly improve his LinkedIn profile.

Elon Musk

Pros:

Musk has created billion-dollar brands in 5 completely different fields, namely: financial services (Zip2 and PayPal); banking (X.com and PayPal); transportation and automotive (Tesla Motors and the Hyperloop Project); energy (SolarCity and Tesla) and; space exploration (Space X).

Musk is unique in that he simultaneously runs three of these, including Tesla, Space X, and SolarCity. While Jobs ran Pixar and Apple simultaneously, he was not as hands-on with both in the same way that Musk is with all of his companies. Musk innovated the payments, automotive, space and solar industries, and all virtually at the same time. Musk focused on product/service rather than brand.

Musk declared a desire to have a greater impact on the future of humanity's destiny and went beyond Gates, with ambitions to create civilisation on MarsMusk. In fact, he built a functioning video game at the age of 12. The game, Blastar, was reportedly sold for $500.

He looked to the future and focused on the existence of humanity to find solutions. He was inspired by what the majority of people wanted/ needed, instead of just focusing on how he could make only his life easier.

Musk allowed all his patents and sources to be opened to the public to copy when he could have made billions by selling them.

Musk is an excellent negotiator, gaining billions of dollars from friends, family, associates, and the government to challenge the status quo when his companies were running out of money; he always found a way to keep funding them.

Cons:

Musk's success would not have been possible without government funding for basic research and subsidies for electric cars and solar panels. Above all, he has benefited from a long series of innovations in batteries, solar cells, and space travel. Musk sells himself as a singular mover of mountains and does not like to share credit for his success.

Musk is known for humiliating engineers and firing employees on a whim. In 2014, when his assistant asked for a raise, the assistant who had devoted her life to Tesla and SpaceX for 12 years, he summarily let her go. Although he wants to focus on humanity's problems, some say he does not really care about the poor/middle class. The business models are an example of this, especially his work with SpaceX and Tesla.

Some critics claim that Musk has a distorted vision of reality, which is a common theme in Vance's book about him. Also, Musk has a very poor LinkedIn profile.

Of course, I could have factored into this discussion the Google founders, Larry Page and Sergey Brin, FaceBook founder, Mark Zuckerberg, Amazon founder, Jeff Bezos, as well as the founders of Skype on this list, among others.

Nevertheless, I felt that the three I have highlighted have had the most disruptive, effective, and innovative ways of using technology, and more so than anyone else, each of them has been a singular founder and innovator in completely new areas, with new inventions, and new ways of working. There was search before Google, there was social before FaceBook, and there was online shopping before Amazon, for example. Arguable I know, but it's merely my view.

So Who Is the Greatest?

So, who do I think is the greatest technology entrepreneur?

Elon Musk.

Why?

Well, I used to love my iPod shuffle for listening to music while cycling. I now use Bluetooth headphones and my Spotify on my Huawei phone, and I was one of the first to own an iPhone in the UK. I have also always used Office until I created my own business. Now, I have the entire company on Google for the sake of simplicity and ease of work.

However, I think what Musk has done in five verticals is incredible. To take on NASA and win is amazing. To take on payments and win is amazing. To create Tesla, which has undoubtedly changed the market of cars, has been outstanding. To then move onto solar energy is phenomenal.

It's not just the areas he has been in, but what he has done in them and the innovative and value-based way he has looked at things, like reusing rockets, which NASA never did. I find that most impressive.

The fact that he is CEO, and a hands-on CEO at that, of Space X, Tesla, and Solar City at the same time, all multibillion-dollar companies, is simply unprecedented. For that and the fact that he is so young and has so much more to come, colonising Mars, for example, means that I think that he is the greatest.

Chapter Twenty-Three

New Year, New Personal Brand

Many people make New Year's resolutions that are well intentioned but fall away. If you want to achieve your business objectives every year, you should focus on developing your personal brand on LinkedIn and beyond, and keep it going throughout the year. It's now more important than ever.

People buy people. Always have, always will. That's why the phrase, 'It's not what you know, it's who you know', is as true now as it was 100 years ago. Today, they are buying your personal brand. Think you don't need a personal brand? Think again.

Here are 13 reasons why you need a personal brand:

1. **You already have a personal brand:** If you don't control it, it's being controlled for you, by other people. Your brand perception is out there of you; you can manage it, or you can let others take it away from you. Your reputation is being managed whether you like it or not. It's better to control it and manage it yourself.

2. **If you want a new job**, then your personal brand will dictate whether you succeed or not after your application. The first thing an HR director or recruiting team does is look at your LinkedIn profile. With no photo, no summary page, and no updated job title/experience, you won't even get an interview.

3. **If you want a promotion in your existing company**, you will stand more chance of getting it with an enhanced personal brand. If your competition for that senior role has more

recommendations on LinkedIn, more blog posts, engages more, has more connections on LinkedIn, and their profile looks better overall, they will beat you to that position. Are their rankings for views higher than yours in the company? Are their LinkedIn ratings higher than that of professionals like you? Where do you stand?

4. **If you want to keep clients**, then you should focus on your personal brand. If you're not and your client is being wooed by another service provider and the other service provider's personal branding on LinkedIn is better than yours, then you may just lose that client. Enhance, engage, and increase your visibility through social selling/marketing on LinkedIn.

5. **If you want to win a client**, then you must enhance your personal brand. If you don't and they look at your LinkedIn profile and see nothing impressive, no thought leadership, no sharing of content, no engagement, no blogs, no connections, and no company page, then social selling indications are that you will miss out and not even know about it.

6. **If you want to impress the media**, then you must show that you are a thought leader and demonstrate your accomplishments through LinkedIn. Talk about the events that you spoke at and have been invited to, and talk about the things that you have done in a business context. It's not boasting; it's factual and it's helping communicate your personal brand values. People also like working with winners and those who influence.

7. **If you want investors**, then you need to give them reasons to invest. People invest in people, just like they employ people or buy from people: because of the person and their personal brand. If you have a fully rounded personal brand on LinkedIn that looks impressive and is backed up with substance as well as style, then you are more likely to: 1) get investors approaching you, and 2) be welcomed with an open door when you approach the investors. Why should someone invest in you if you can't invest in yourself personally?

8. **If you want to reassure shareholders** and keep them informed about what you're doing and how well you're doing, then having a personal brand that is full of confidence and updates on LinkedIn is key. Blog about your successes, let people know about your innovations and direction. Educate, inform, inspire.

9. **If you want to be an event speaker of any kind**, from speaking for a company at an event to speaking at a conference, then you need to give the organiser of that event the confidence to employ you. If your personal brand on LinkedIn contains no speaking engagements, no details of when you chaired an event successfully, or no recommendations from other event organisers, then why should a future event organiser employ you?

   Add pictures, videos of you in action, and list all of the events that you have done and are doing. Confidence is everything in event speaking, for the organisers as well as the speakers. That confidence comes from a confident personal brand. Keyword search will also determine whether you get found or not. If you don't list what you have done speaking-wise, then how do you expect people to find you and know you're any good at speaking?

10. **If you want to blog for a media brand**, then you have to demonstrate that you have the credibility and the following to make a publisher allow you to blog for them and be exposed to their audience. They have to want you to publish for them. List your writing experience and blogging experience on your personal brand on your LinkedIn profile.

11. **Employer branding:** People work for leaders with an enhanced personal brand. If you want employees in places like Singapore (where there is virtually full employment), or you want to keep existing employees, then you have to have a personal brand worth following.

   All great leaders have great personal brands. In the Digital Age, LinkedIn has become a primary means of projecting your personal brand. In a competitive world, you need to impress and inspire your employees into seeing that you're worth working for and that you are worth staying with, and you need to impress future employees that you're worth following. A great personal brand can tick so many boxes when it comes to this. Give people reasons to see that they can learn from you and that you are worth following.

12. **If you want to be recommended and referred to by others**, then you need a personal brand on LinkedIn that is worth showing to other people. Remember: Your LinkedIn personal profile never sleeps; it's being viewed 24/7 by people all around the world. Try Googling your name. What comes up first? Your LinkedIn profile.

    Worth thinking about. (PS: Try Googling your company and what comes up first or second? Your LinkedIn company page. Even more frightening is when you see some company pages, MNCs and SMEs. All that hard work on your website is blown away because you have no updates on your LinkedIn company page.)

13. **If you want to be head-hunted**, it goes without saying that you need a great personal brand on LinkedIn that contains all your achievements, awards, associations, companies you have worked for, promotions you have gained, and innovative things that you have done.

If you don't, then there are plenty of other people on LinkedIn whom a head-hunter can move onto who will show all their achievements and give reasons why they should be picked because of the way that they have communicated their personal brand on LinkedIn. With no keywords, you won't even get found in the first place.

In summary, you are in charge of your own personal branding. If you wish to achieve great things in the business world, LinkedIn is the first place that this starts. If you don't look after your own personal brand, you are more likely to fail in your ambitions, and your competitors are more likely to win. If you do, you are more likely to win and succeed in your business objectives, whatever they are.

Don't forget that you get the same space on LinkedIn as Richard Branson or Bill Gates, and your company gets the same space as Google or Apple. It's up to you to make that space work effectively for you and rise above the competition. Anyone can do it. You can too. Good luck with achieving your business objectives. Happy New Personal Brand!

Chapter Twenty-Four

Summary—Using Personal Branding in Your Career

While I was in Sydney conducting the sold-out first Sydney date of my Global Rock Star Profile Tour, I met with the amazing and inspirational Jane Jackson. It was a classic case of networking first on LinkedIn, meeting virtually, building a relationship, and then meeting in real life—something that I am very passionate about. I don't believe that you need to meet people first before connecting with them. Sorry, LinkedIn!

Jane very kindly offered to interview me for her insightful and compelling podcast on her website, and I was lucky to be number 110! Congratulations, Jane, on a great series of podcasts.

Read my interview transcription below, which talks about my favourite subject, LinkedIn, and how you can use it to achieve all your business objectives, personal branding, employer branding, content marketing, thought leadership, and lead generation/creating new business. Cheers, Jane!

Interview: LinkedIn Book, LinkedIn Mastery for Entrepreneurs

Speaker 1: Welcome to the Publisher Book podcast, where we speak with authors from around the world to find out how they transformed their dream into a published reality. Here's your host, Adam Ashton.

Adam Ashton: I've just spoken with Chris J. Reed, the author of *LinkedIn Mastery for Entrepreneurs.* Now, that book is one of 55,000 books about LinkedIn on Amazon, and this is the number one: the number one best LinkedIn book out there. That's an impressive title in itself.

Chris Reed is the founder and CEO of Black Marketing, which is a NASDAQ-listed LinkedIn marketing company focusing on getting people's LinkedIn right, making LinkedIn effective, and using it to really build your personal brand. We start this conversation with the absolute basics of what LinkedIn is, and we ramp it up through all the things that you need to have in your profile, how to fix your profile, and towards the end, we talk about some of the paid premium services like Sales Navigator, which sounds absolutely amazing. I've never used it before.

I think if you listen to this, take some notes on how you can improve your LinkedIn profile. If you're not on LinkedIn, absolutely get on it, for sure. I need to quickly go away and fix my LinkedIn profile because there's plenty of things I'm doing wrong. Enjoy this conversation with Chris J. Reed, the only NASDAQ-listed CEO with a Mohawk, the author of *LinkedIn Mastery for Entrepreneurs*.

You ready to get stuck in?

Chris J. Reed: Yep, I am indeed.

Adam Ashton: Fantastic. Today I'm with Chris J. Reed, the absolute LinkedIn master. Chris, thanks for joining me. Can you tell everyone a little bit about yourself?

Chris J. Reed: Sure. I'm Chris J. Reed. I'm the only CEO with a Mohawk, and the only NASDAQ-listed CEO with a Mohawk. Today, it's red.

Adam Ashton: I was going to say red.

Chris J. Reed: It's red. It's red today, and it's blue on my book. I had the blue because LinkedIn blue ties into the book. We do personal branding, we do company branding, we do social selling. We make thought leaders on LinkedIn of CEOs and entrepreneurs across the world.

We have many clients in Melbourne, in Sydney, and other parts of Australia, but also in places like Singapore, Shanghai, and Hong Kong, and I'm currently in New York; we have clients over here. We have clients in America, we have clients in Europe as well. It's very much a global phenomenon about how I can use LinkedIn to enhance your personal branding.

Adam Ashton: Fantastic. I don't know too many LinkedIn experts, but every time, I just see Chris J. Reed everywhere.

Chris J. Reed: That's the idea, mate.

Adam Ashton: Yeah. The other thing is, you seem to be in a different city every week as well.

Chris J. Reed: I was in Melbourne last week, so yes, you're right. I actually got off a plane Saturday morning from Melbourne to Singapore where I live, where my headquarters is. Then I literally got a plane the next day to New York. We have our founders' meeting here. I've got a week of meetings and workshops and that kind of thing here before I go back to Singapore next week. I much prefer Singapore. I have to say it's too damn cold here.

Adam Ashton: Yeah, for sure, but . . . I know you said you started in about 2014, with just you and your laptop.

Chris J. Reed: That's it.

We have about 100 clients, and we're quite selective about who we take on because, one, they need to be able to afford us, and two, they need to actually understand the benefits of doing LinkedIn. Which is something a lot of people just don't get.

Adam Ashton: Yeah.

Chris J. Reed: Don't understand it at all. They think they can do it themselves, and they can't basically.

Adam Ashton: Yeah, for sure. I just realised, we're a couple of minutes in, and I haven't even said the title of your book. *LinkedIn Mastery for Entrepreneurs* . . .

Chris J. Reed: Indeed. The best-selling book about LinkedIn in the world. Amazon told me that. Of the 55,000 books about LinkedIn, written on amazon.com, *LinkedIn Mastery for Entrepreneurs* is actually number one. I've actually got screen shots of me beating people like Donald Trump and Elon Musk and Steve Jobs.

Adam Ashton: That's awesome.

Chris J. Reed: And that's fine with me.

Adam Ashton: That's absolutely awesome. Well, let's . . . I reckon we'll start the LinkedIn conversation at a very basic level and ramp our way up, so at the most basic level, what is LinkedIn if anyone doesn't know what it is yet?

Chris J. Reed: LinkedIn is basically a peer-to-peer network in a business context. It's basically FaceBook for business. It's really important people understand that it's not a place you can be anonymous. You have to put your company name on there. You have to advertise to people who you are, and basically everyone knows who you are. Everyone knows people who know who you are, so you can't be derogatory and you can't be anonymous.

You have to actually think about what you say. You have to think about how you come across both from your personal brand point of view, but also your company point of view. It makes people think about what they share, what they say, and what they do. You get more civilised debate on LinkedIn as a result of it, and it's more of a business context than is something like FaceBook or Twitter.

Adam Ashton: Very nice. How many people are on LinkedIn? Obviously, it's growing all the time . . .

Chris J. Reed: 550 million in the world and, interestingly, Australia accounts for about 10 million people, for example. It's quite saturated when it comes to professionals in Asia, Asia Pacific where I spend most of my time (i.e., Singapore). When I first came there eight years ago, there were 10 million people on LinkedIn. Now, there's 110 million people across Asia Pacific.

It's quite phenomenal how that's grown, but the reason why we do a lot of business in Australia and New Zealand is because they obviously got it first. They were about the second or third country, behind the UK and America, to really understand LinkedIn and get LinkedIn, and they've been using LinkedIn for a while now. It's just that they also need help in terms of how to take it from being a recruitment tool and a CV tool to being a social selling tool, a lead generation tool, an employer branding tool, a personal branding tool, and a content marketing tool.

That's where we come in. We basically show you how to do it, and if you don't want to buy our services, that's up to you. You can read the book, you can come to my workshop, pick up tips, and go away and do it yourself. If you want to take my services, that's also fine as well, so it's very much a win-win because we know if we give information away, such as things out of the book and the workshops, then people will, basically, say, 'Oh yeah, Black Marketing are the people that you need to go to for your LinkedIn expertise and your LinkedIn marketing', should you have the budget to do so, should you wish to do so.

Adam Ashton: Fantastic. That sounds awesome. So, you gave a whole list of things of what people could do. What are some of the biggest opportunities on LinkedIn and what are most people missing, because I'd say most people know nothing . . . ?

Chris J. Reed: I totally agree. Basically, lead generation is the one thing that people don't know they can do on LinkedIn. It's the personal branding; you have to get your personal branding right. You have to get your picture right, your background, headline, and your summary section, and then, you have to start being a thought leader. Start sharing content, start writing content and relevant content in a business context about your business, about Australia, about the economy, about innovation, about technology, and then basically, you can use the Sales Navigator platform to really find people to the Nth degree.

I can find any entrepreneurs. Like, last week, I was in Melbourne, and I had 35 meetings. Thirty-five meetings were set up with entrepreneurs whom I found on LinkedIn. I sent them a nice note to say I'm just doing Melbourne this week, do you want to have a meeting to talk about your LinkedIn? We then qualified the meeting and got down to 35 people, and we sold out two workshops as a result of it, on top of the 35 meetings. I had effectively 50 meetings last week; plus I did two paid for talks: one with the American Chamber of Commerce and one with a couple of other organisations.

The thirst for information is just phenomenal, and it all came through me targeting people on LinkedIn. I found them on LinkedIn, I used the data on LinkedIn, I found entrepreneurs or founders on LinkedIn, and I wrote them a short message saying, 'I want to talk to you', and they said yes, and that's the amazing thing about LinkedIn. I can find anybody, anywhere in the world: America, Melbourne, Shanghai, Singapore, Hong Kong, Europe. I can find them all through using the data on LinkedIn.

Adam Ashton: That sounds awesome, and I'm definitely keen to . . . Yeah, definitely kind of get stuck into a bit of that because there's a lot of stuff that I don't even know about, that I was reading through the book, not that I'm by any means a LinkedIn expert but . . . A lot of people, probably early on, thought LinkedIn was for people looking for a job or for HR departments looking for new employees, but that's not true anymore, is it?

Chris J. Reed: No, not at all. It's very much gone away from that: Recruitment is still the number one way that LinkedIn makes money, but it has really changed. Sales Navigator came on board two or three years ago, and that's the lead generation tool. The publishing platform came on board, so you can basically write blogs. You can become a thought leader. You can share content, and you can do employer branding too.

It's all about how you make your company attractive to employees but also investors, clients, and future employees. It's really the Sales Navigator platform that's transformed LinkedIn from being about CVs and data to being about, 'Well, if I can find someone to do a job, I can find them to become client'. That's really the crux of what you do, but it only works if you've got a very good personal brand, lots of connections, a good content marketing strategy, a good employment branding strategy, and a good company branding strategy.

People stay on the LinkedIn app. They like to use the phone and not go away from the phone, so they stay on the phone looking at your content, looking at your connections, looking at who you know, looking at your experience, looking at your thought leadership, and then they decide to respond to you, or they approach you because of things like keywords, or being found on keywords, and that's the key. LinkedIn is just like Google. You get found by using certain keywords. If you use the right keywords, you get found.

Adam Ashton: Very nice. Very nice. And, LinkedIn ranks extremely highly on Google, doesn't it?

Chris J. Reed: Phenomenally high. Let's see, if I google you, Adam, one of the first things that comes up is your LinkedIn profile.

Adam Ashton: Yeah.

Chris J. Reed: And the first thing then is the impression I get of you if I click on that. The first impression I get of you is your LinkedIn profile, and people often completely misunderstand this and misuse this and think, 'Oh no, people won't find me on LinkedIn'. We will because you just have to google you to find you. Plus, if I look at your LinkedIn, I can find you, but more importantly, if I google you, your LinkedIn profile comes above your FaceBook, above your YouTube, above your website, above everything else.

Your LinkedIn profile comes up number one. And that's the first impression that someone gets of you. If you're looking for a job, or if you want to find an investment, or you want to find employees or clients, you have to think, 'How does this come across to them?' because, believe me, they're all googling you to see what you're like.

It's the most obvious thing in the world. I'm on the way to a meeting, or think about applying to somebody. The first thing you do is google them and then see what they're like, and the first thing that comes up is your LinkedIn profile, and people just completely underestimate the power of this, but it's just logical if you think about it. Google is very powerful. LinkedIn is very powerful. The two together are even more powerful.

Adam Ashton: Nice, so you said for entrepreneurs there's a lot of lead generation. We'll get into the Sales Navigator a little bit later, but you said it's a big, massive publishing platform and basically probably some personal branding.

Chris J. Reed: Right.

Adam Ashton: Aside from LinkedIn, what else should people be focusing on? Let's start with what would you define as personal branding? What is someone's personal brand?

Chris J. Reed: Good question. My personal brand is obviously the Mohawk and it's about being an entrepreneur and it's about being on LinkedIn and it's about doing the talks and the authorship and being an entrepreneur in both the UK, where I first started, then Singapore, eight years ago, and being a global leader when it comes to an authority about LinkedIn and how to use LinkedIn.

I've got the number one profile in Australia. I've got the number one profile in Singapore, and the number one profile in Hong Kong. I make sure that in all the markets where we have business, we have the number one profile. We're the top social selling index, which is basically how LinkedIn measures whether you're a top social seller or not.

I beat everybody who works for LinkedIn in Australia on social selling to the degree that when I met a guy, when I was down there last week, he looked at my social selling index and went, 'Jesus, how did you get 94? That's impossible. Nobody on my team at LinkedIn have got more than 82'. I said, 'I'm actually using the platform. I use it 24/7 a day. I bet most of your team aren't', and he went, 'Oh, yes, probably not'.

They just sell it. I don't understand it. They sell it, but they don't actually use LinkedIn as a platform to market their own services. I know it's totally ironic.

Also, half our clients are marketing agencies or social agencies or creative agencies who are phenomenal at doing great jobs for their clients, but absolutely terrible at marketing themselves. Really, really bad at marketing themselves, partly because they don't have time and partly because no one's paying them. Marketing agencies have this thing, which is a bit like lawyers. If no one's paying them, they won't do anything.

Adam Ashton: Yeah, sure.

Chris J. Reed: No one's paying them to do their own stuff. They go, 'I'm not going to do this. I could do some clients' stuff and earn some money, or do it myself', without realising that it's actually counterproductive because it comes back to you. Because you then ask them, 'Well, how do you generate leads?' and they say, 'Well, it's all through referrals'; you go, 'Well, that's nice as long as the referral keeps on coming. What happens when the referrals stop?' They say, 'Ah, that's a good point'.

Well, that's where LinkedIn comes in because then you could have both. You can have referrals, and you could have a proactive pipeline. I'd much rather have the destiny in my own hands and actually be reaching out to people and having a pipeline than purely relying on next week, twiddling my thumbs going, 'Is somebody going to refer me this week? Is someone going to refer to me next week?' I'd rather be proactive and be positive and be aggressive, in a positive way, in a targeted way, and say to people, like I did last week in Melbourne, 'You know I'm here, let's have a chat'.

We probably picked up maybe four or five clients as a result of the meetings last week, which is absolutely phenomenal, and we inspired other people to use LinkedIn, inspired other people to also do things like blogging and taking pictures and telling other people about it, which is part of what we do. It's the word-of-mouth side of things, which LinkedIn is very powerful for too.

Adam Ashton: Very nice. Just quickly, on personal branding, aside from LinkedIn, and then we'll come straight back to LinkedIn. What else should we include in our personal branding, aside from LinkedIn? Is there anything else we need?

Chris J. Reed: Yeah. I definitely think that. One of the reasons I talked about the book is the book is very much about my personal branding. For instance, my publisher advised against putting my picture on the front cover. Nobody puts a picture of themselves on their book, and sure enough, if you look at business books, hardly anybody's got their picture on it. I said, 'But you miss the point. Part of my personal brand is the Mohawk, so if I don't put the Mohawk on the front cover, it just becomes another book about LinkedIn. I put it on the front cover and automatically, it stands out on the shelf, which then proves my point about personal branding'.

Literally, I could walk down, and I've had stories where I'd walk down streets; say I've been to an art gallery in Shanghai and some guy I have never met before comes up to me and says, 'You don't know me, but we are connected on LinkedIn. I recognise you because of your Mohawk'.

I met a guy in a lift in Hong Kong in the mall, and he said, 'Oh, you did a talk three years ago in Hong Kong at the British Chamber of Commerce about LinkedIn, and I recognised you because of your Mohawk'. I met a guy in the airport in Shanghai and the same thing. I obviously meet people in Singapore all the time, but it's happened in Sydney, it's happened in Melbourne, literally everywhere I go. It stands out.

That's what I think is very important. Things like the book work, and then things like YouTube work. We do lots and lots of interviews, lots and lots of contributions like this, lots of podcasts, lots of radio interviews. Australia, I think is particularly good when it comes to things like TV interviews, podcasts, and radio interviews. They do a much better job than maybe Northern Asia does, for example. It's all about kind of sharing this content and sharing my passion for LinkedIn with other people as well, which is part of our USP; it's part of our personal branding.

I think YouTube plays a part in this. For example, I have lots of my podcasts on my YouTube channel. I'll put this on my YouTube channel as well. I'll share this, obviously, on LinkedIn as well, and we have all the interviews on my YouTube channel. The great thing about YouTube is that you can share it on LinkedIn, and people can watch the video on LinkedIn. You don't have to leave LinkedIn, so we have lots of videos on our company page, on my personal page, on LinkedIn. If you look at the app, on LinkedIn, on the mobile, you can watch the video in the app and then move on to another part of LinkedIn.

You don't have to actually leave LinkedIn to go somewhere else. People don't like leaving. They like to stay. Whether it's FaceBook, whether it's LinkedIn, whether it's Instagram, they don't want to leave, so basically you have to work within the parameters of LinkedIn itself and make sure the content that people want to see about us is actually on LinkedIn itself.

Adam Ashton: Fantastic. So, basically for anyone wanting to build a personal brand, LinkedIn, YouTube, maybe a book if they can, and get a Mohawk . . . ?

Chris J. Reed: Definitely. Get a different kind of Mohawk. I met a guy yesterday who had a beard as long as my Mohawk. Literally, he had nothing on top. I have the Mohawk, he has the beard down here, so it's like, well, geez; it's very funny. At least dye it red, and then we can have both.

Adam Ashton: How long does it take you to do your Mohawk?

Chris J. Reed: It takes me five minutes because it's obviously been cut this way, and I've been growing it for several years. It takes me literally five minutes, but I have to use clay, because I live in Singapore, and it's 80% humidity most of the time, and 25 degrees Celsius is the lowest it gets. The average temperature is about 34, 35. You have to use clay. If you use anything but clay, it falls over because the humidity attacks it. You need clay to make sure it stays up. I'll tell you, it's very testy because we have torrential rain, and it's so humid. It's very testy.

Adam Ashton: Love it.

Chris J. Reed: I think about all these things, Adam. Things I never thought I'd have to think about 10 years ago. I get asked great questions by men like you now about my hair, and I have these bizarre conversations with grown-up men about hair colouring and hair products and this kind of thing. It's very strange conversations I have now.

Adam Ashton: You said you go red, you go blue. Do you go anything else? Any other bizarre colours?

Chris J. Reed: Oh, yes. I have a lot of pictures of me. Turquoise, green, red, yellow, pink. What did I have the other day? I had blonde. I probably chose red because of the Chinese year, the rooster. We're basically being a rooster, but also, the blue works very well. Blue is actually quite hard because it basically stays blue for about two days, and then it just washes out. It's very hard to keep that LinkedIn blue.

It goes turquoise, and then it goes this kind of weird green colour. Red is actually easy, but even the red goes kind of pink and then it goes white and then it goes . . . You know, you have to do it every two weeks. It's really no fun, I'm intentional with my Mohawk, Adam.

Adam Ashton: Well, that's it. It's part of your personal brand. You're locked in now.

Chris J. Reed: I'm locked in. Somebody said to me the other day, 'What happens if you start losing your hair, or if you change your mind'? I said, 'I can't. I can't change my mind; I can't lose my hair. It has to stay there forever'.

Adam Ashton: Love it. OK, let's get stuck into some of the elements of a good LinkedIn profile. Chapter six, your book, 'Mastering Your LinkedIn Profile Like A Pro'. First things first: the photo. What do we need to do with our photo?

Chris J. Reed: Don't have a FaceBook photograph because FaceBook photographs are the number one way of not being treated seriously on LinkedIn. It's a business photograph, don't forget. You think about how you want to come across in that business context, and that's how you want to come across on LinkedIn, so it needs to be basically a professional photograph, but it also needs to convey your character.

You also have to remember, on LinkedIn, it's very, very small. It's very small, it's circular, and on the app, it's quite small as well. So, you have to think about it. You can't put too much into it. It's very small. I deliberately use a red background, and then I use my book cover, so it's black, and then it's blue because I know it stands out. I've tried various different things in it, but you can't really tell a story about it at all, so that's very important.

The background picture: You can tell a story. At the moment, I have one up of New York, but last week it was of Melbourne. I had a list of all the dates I was doing in Melbourne, and I had a nice picture of Melbourne. I had a picture of the tour, which we call the Rock Star Profile Tour in Melbourne, for example.

I had all this in the background because you can do a lot more with a background picture. People underestimate the background picture. You have all this space apart from the middle bit where you can really talk about your brand, company, and really go for it.

The next most important thing is actually the headline, and you can manipulate the headline by using keywords. We use things like 'LinkedIn', 'entrepreneur', 'Mohawk', 'CEO', 'social media', 'B2B', etc., etc., so we're always using keywords. We're really pushing the boundaries of what LinkedIn will allow. LinkedIn basically has given a space to do a name, but I basically use the name to do my branding, the Mohawk, Black Marketing . . . I don't know if anyone reading this has realised, but they actually put in an area now, where you can put your maiden name.

Obviously, guys don't have a maiden name. I went, 'Ah, right, great, more space'. Now, I have in my maiden name space 'Black Marketing Enabling LinkedIn for You' or 'Social Media Guru' or 'LinkedIn Guru' or 'Entrepreneur with a Mohawk'. This kind of thing. I'm now using that space to basically fill a gap. They didn't have that in the old LinkedIn. They have it in new LinkedIn.

Then, of course, you have to do a nice summary section. The summary section is all about your personal branding. It's really about your story. A lot of people do it in the third person, but really it should be done in the first person because it's like this, we're having a conversation. I would never say to you, Adam, 'Chris said this' and 'Chris said that', because you would think I was a weirdo.

I say, 'I do and don't do that on LinkedIn', because you do come across as a complete idiot if you start saying, 'Chris did this' and 'Chris did that' on LinkedIn. People say, 'Either his PA wrote this or he's talking about himself in the third party', and even if your PA did write it, don't let that come across. You have to be personal; it's one-on-one, so it has to be in the first person.

Adam Ashton: Sure.

Chris J. Reed: It has to be your story as well. A lot of people put in their summary section about their jobs and really that should be about 10%. Most of it should be about what made you a great leader, what makes you interested in business, what do you do in business, what awards have you won, what are you passionate about, what do you do when you're away from your job? Do you mentor students? Do you do voluntary work? Have you won awards? Have you lived in different countries? All these kinds of things, but in a business context.

Then adding things like visuals and video, that kind of thing, really beefs up your profile too, and all of this helps you, basically, get found on LinkedIn through optimisation as well.

Adam Ashton: Very nice. How long should their summary section be, do you reckon?

Chris J. Reed: You have to allow 2,000 characters.

Adam Ashton: Yeah.

Chris J. Reed: Which sounds like a lot, but it's not. It really is not a lot of characters. Basically, only about 10 sentences. Ten or 12 sentences. It's really about you saying, 'I used to do this and I did this, and now

I do this and I'm interested in doing this, and I go forward and do this'. It fills it out quite easily.

Then, your company page section should be basically a replica of your company page section itself. You'd really be copying and pasting it to ensure planned brand consistency, and the problem with the company section, if you leave the employee to actually do it themselves, is that they will always say what they do at the company, which is really boring, because they will say, 'I make the tea at Black Marketing'. Everyone goes, 'I don't care about the tea at Black Marketing. I care what Black Marketing can do for me'.

Adam Ashton: For sure.

Chris J. Reed: That's why we enforce, at Black Marketing, everyone has to copy and paste the company page, and our company page says that's what we do for other people.

A lot of people don't realise that LinkedIn's external, not internal. It's like your website. If your website is designed by marketing to optimise and to be found and to say what you do, your LinkedIn should be the same, but a lot of people don't do this because they don't enforce it on employees to say, 'Actually you represent the company, and it's outward bound and external', so, therefore, you have to represent the company in a positive way and say what the company can actually do for a client or a partner or for somebody else. Not what you do at that company.

Even if you're the managing director, like I didn't even put in the fact that I'm the CEO on my description. I'd like to write about what Black Marketing can do for other CEOs, other founders. Basically, I put in the title, CEO, and obviously people know what a CEO is, but if I started talking about the day-to-day of what I do, all the HR, the operational stuff, and taking on new business, nobody cares.

They care what we can do for them, and that's the fundamental point people don't understand. Probably about 10% of the profiles on LinkedIn describe what they can do externally and about 90% say what they can do internally.

Adam Ashton: Yeah, for sure. In terms of that experience section as well, what experience should we be putting down there? Obviously, we don't want to say, 'When I was 18, I worked in a pub', or anything like that.

Chris J. Reed: Well, you can say that, you see: I'll give you an example. I mentor SMU students in Singapore Management University who are taking marketing degrees, and, I say to them, 'Put all of your internal experience and all of your external experience on there because it builds up a picture of someone who's actually hard-working'.

If you've got three or four internships or summer jobs, for example, and then your competition for that same job has nothing because they travelled the world or basically did nothing, they stayed at home with their parents or they basically did nothing for that summer, you stand out. Because, you look like you're working hard.

I mean personally, as soon as I was 16, I got a Saturday job at HMV, I got a weekend job at HMV, I got a weekday job at HMV, I did my summer holiday at HMV, and it is probably because I was passionate about music, but also because I wanted to earn some money and I wanted to learn about commerce and marketing, and I knew, by working there at a Saturday job and a weekend job and a summer job, I could go down to the marketing department in London and learn about how you did marketing for HMV. Which, as a 16-year-old, is fantastic. Obviously, it's the music industry as well, so even better.

The point is, I put that on my LinkedIn and still, to this day, it's on my LinkedIn, because it builds up my character in terms of the fact that I believe in hard work, I believe in going out there and doing things. I mentor students to do the same thing. The ones that do internships, the ones that stand out by saying, 'I have a Saturday job', the ones that did work in the pub when they were 18 years old and actually proved they were able to handle customers and talk about business and create relationships. These people actually do stand out. Putting in things like that is very relevant.

Adam Ashton: OK. Nice.

Chris J. Reed: Another thing you should put down is also things about experience, like I'm a board director of the British Chamber of Commerce, for example, in Singapore, so I put that on there. I'm also a mentor of SMU students at Singapore Management University, so I put that on there. I also do things with my brother, so I put that on there. All the things that are linked to a business section you can add on there because if you don't, you can't get found.

What this means is . . . I'm a board director, I can approach the chamber in Melbourne and say to them, 'Can I do a talk with you about doing LinkedIn'? and they can then check me out, they can find me, they can check out who I know. But I can also find them.

Adam Ashton: Nice.

Chris J. Reed: I find them through LinkedIn, they can find me through LinkedIn, but also, more importantly, Singapore Chamber can find me and reach out to me, and say, 'What's it like being part of the Chamber?' or 'Can you help me with this?' or whatever it happens to be. I can reach out to other chambers across the world because of the same thing.

It's all about communication, but it's all about in the business context, so that's why I've got about 50 different positions because I'm quite involved in lots of communities, lots of professional organisations within Singapore and Hong Kong and basically Australia. I believe in putting that all on my LinkedIn. Experience doesn't just mean your job; it means anything to do with a business context.

Adam Ashton: Very nice. OK, cool. Maybe I need to put a few more things on there. Some of the other things . . . That's basically your profile, is that right? I'm just trying to figure out, am I missing anything?

Chris J. Reed: Yeah. That's the main thing, but what also goes onto your profile is your thought leadership and your content marketing.

Adam Ashton: Fantastic. I've got one quick question. The background picture: Can anyone do that?

Chris J. Reed: Everyone should do that.

Adam Ashton: Oh, really? I didn't even know you could do it.

Chris J. Reed: Everyone, please do it; if you don't do it . . . Well, on yours, I had a quick look at yours, and I don't think you've got one.

Adam Ashton: No, I think I'm the classic LinkedIn blue.

Chris J. Reed: LinkedIn now give every single person a background picture. Yes, you've got the LinkedIn blue. They give everyone that because they're encouraging you to put your own background picture there, so you can have your entrepreneur bookings or your podcast or something like that and the branding there. You're missing out on an opportunity to market your business on there, and everyone is as well. Lots of people have got that blue background because they're not realising that's a very powerful platform.

You can see that on the mobile, on the tablet, on the laptop, everywhere. Basically, you're missing out on an opportunity to market yourselves, and it's free. It's completely free. All you have to do is design a picture that's that size, which is relatively simple to do, and put it up there and then you're marketing because everyone has to come to your profile. Everyone who comes to your profile sees that straightaway. It's very powerful.

Adam Ashton: Nice. How does it go with . . . You say you can see it on the mobile as well. Obviously, it's a very different size. How does the sizing work out . . . ?

Chris J. Reed: Oh well, that's a good question actually because the sizing is slightly different, and I complained to LinkedIn about this.

Adam Ashton: Yeah.

Chris J. Reed: This morning, I talked to a good woman on LinkedIn and said to them, 'You do realise that your picture for your mobile is different-sized to your picture for your laptop and your tablet'? They hadn't realised because, again, they don't use it. No one had actually said to them, 'You do realise this is completely different'. I mean, it would be OK if they actually gave you the opportunity to upload a different picture for different platform, but they don't. You basically ensure it stands out on a mobile. It's just a bit of tweaking.

Adam Ashton: Nice.

Chris J. Reed: Hopefully, they might give the opportunity in the future to upload three different pictures, one for your tablet, one for your laptop, one for your mobile, but until that happens, you've got to basically get the pictures sized just right, to make sure you can see it in all of them, and then you've got an interesting experiment. You've got to put it in, load it up, and then check it out on the mobile, check it out on the tablet, and check it out on your laptop.

Adam Ashton: Fantastic. OK, yeah, cool. Yeah, nice. As you see, I'm just your classic LinkedIn blue. I need to get on to that. All right. Cool. We're going to talk about content marketing. You said, first things first, you need to make a content marketing plan.

Chris J. Reed: Definitely.

Adam Ashton: And, what does that plan involve? You said there is created content and curated content.

Chris J. Reed: Correct, so created content is blogging. When you blog on LinkedIn, which is the biggest publishing platform in the world, it's your thoughts about a subject. When this podcast goes out, I'll do a blog about that, for example. I did a blog last week. I got coverage in the Business Times in Singapore and then interviewed six of the people there, so I did a blog about that.

Previously, I did a blog about Singapore Airlines versus Emirates Airlines, the benefits from the business point of view, who is better, who is better from the business perspective. I'm constantly doing blogs that are interesting to my audience and my peers, but also things that I think can go viral and things that people are interested in for their business context that I can show on LinkedIn.

That's a blogging one. Now, it's quite hard to do that every single week or every single fortnight. I understand people say that it takes a long time, and it does. A good blog takes two or three hours to actually do. Sometimes longer. Sometimes you can only do that every few weeks. You have to combine that with a curated content plan, which should be content that you're interested in and your peers are interested in from the content point of view, and not just things about your business.

LinkedIn has a strategy, which is called a 4-1-1 strategy. For every post about your own business, or something related to your business, like my business would be about LinkedIn, do one soft sell post, maybe about social media, and then four completely unrelated posts about other things that have nothing to do with your business.

I could write about Australia. I could write about innovation. I could write about Asia. I could write about marketing. I could write about research trends. I could write about technology, but nothing to do with LinkedIn, and that enables people to appreciate that you're actually sharing interesting things that are relevant to them, and then when you hit them with a hard sell post about your business, they're more likely to then see it and take it up. Because the problem is, if all you do is you push out your company, they will switch off. They'll stop following you, they'll close your feed down, and you won't get across your hard sell pitch when you come to it because they've basically switched off.

You have to appreciate the fact it's a bit like a newspaper. If you go to the newspaper and you just read about your company the whole time, you wouldn't buy it, but if you read about other things, you're more likely to read things interesting in your company as well. It's a combination. That's why it's called 4-1-1. That's what it means about actually coming up with a content marketing strategy.

We come up with a content calendar for our clients, for example, which enables them to see how we separate content and spread content throughout the week, but that also means you have to like, you have to share, and you have to comment on other people's content. You can't just be taking all the time. You've got to be giving something out there, which means that you're sharing their content with your followers. You're commenting on their content to make that go viral and give a contribution away, for example. It's not just one way. It's got to be two ways. It's conversation, but it's a conversation on a massive scale although it's still one-on-one.

Adam Ashton: Mm-hmm (affirmative). For sure. For sure. Obviously, if someone else is reading someone else's thing, let's say you put an interesting comment . . .

Chris J. Reed: They might connect.

Adam Ashton: Yeah. Nice.

Chris J. Reed: Correct. That especially happens when you have the right keywords in your title. If I comment on something, for example, that says, 'Chris Reed, LinkedIn Guru', then people go, 'Oh, that's interesting. I'm looking for someone to do my LinkedIn profile. I'll look at Chris's profile and see if he's any good, see who he knows, see what his recommendations are like, see if he's got any awards, see what his company does, and so forth'.

Adam Ashton: Yeah, for sure. Yeah, very nice. OK, cool. In terms of creating your own content, the blogging, have you got anything specific to LinkedIn for that or is that sort of a bit more personal?

Chris J. Reed: Yeah. Have an opinion. The worst blogs on LinkedIn are people that don't have opinions. You've got to have an opinion, and then, it doesn't matter if you get a lot of abuse because LinkedIn abuse is quite civilised abuse or you get half people saying, 'Yeah'. Basically, you've got to get people commenting, liking, sharing. And people will be both disagreeing with you and agreeing with you.

Basically, I've always failed if I put a blog up there and no one's commented or no one's disagreed with me. I've failed if no one disagrees with me. I much prefer to incite some debate, like I did with my blog about the Emirates versus Singapore Airlines. I knew that was going to polarise opinion.

I basically said that Emirates is terrible and Singapore is fantastic. I had a lot of people going, 'No, that's not true', and I think this other brand is better . . . People say, 'Yes, Singapore is fantastic'. There's this whole debate going on about whether I was right, whether I was wrong: you know, the pros and cons of other airlines, and so forth. That's what you should do. Stimulate people to have a debate; if you don't do that, you've failed in your content marketing strategy.

Adam Ashton: Very nice. You talked about the 4-1-1 rule. There was also the 1-9-90 rule in that 1% of people are creating new content, 9% are maybe sharing it, and 90% are just looking.

Chris J. Reed: Correct. That's very much LinkedIn, and that's very much social media in general. FaceBook, LinkedIn, Instagram, but LinkedIn particularly. You do get about 1% of the people actually creating, 9% sharing and commenting, and 90% just viewing. That's just the way social media is.

Adam Ashton: Yeah, for sure.

Chris J. Reed: Be the 1%.

Adam Ashton: Exactly. Be that 1%. OK, cool. Was there anything else on content marketing? Then, we'll get into social selling.

Chris J. Reed: No, that's plenty. It's not rocket science. It's part of social selling because if you share content, you get people to come to your profile and come to you by sharing valuable content. That's all about social selling. You're doing it in a subtle way. You're selling your services in a subtle way by bringing people to your profile, bringing people to your company, by giving away content.

Adam Ashton: Yeah, fantastic. Can you give us a quick overview of what social selling is?

Chris J. Reed: Social selling is using social media to sell. That's basically it, and basically LinkedIn is the best way of doing that because you can tell who you're selling to. You can obviously do with things like FaceBook and Instagram and YouTube as well, but the trouble with that is, the data isn't there. Whereas, on LinkedIn, I can tell exactly who I'm talking to.

I can tell exactly who I'm connecting with, exactly who is interested in what I actually do. I connect with CEOs, founders, and SMEs, for example, in Melbourne or Victoria or in Sydney, for example, and I share relevant content with them. It becomes social selling.

I also can bring people to me by reaching out with Sales Navigator, and Sales Navigator has been designed to find anyone anywhere in the world using the data on LinkedIn. It's the same data you input, and it is the data that I can access to find you. That's absolutely crucial when it comes to that because that enables me to reach out to somebody. They can check out my profile, they can check out who we both know, they can check out my background picture in my headline, my company page, my blogging, and then they will decide whether to respond or not. That's absolutely crucial, and that's part of social selling too.

It's very much a two-way thing. You can't force people to respond, but you stimulate them to respond and you give them enough reason to respond, and they will do, but sharing content is actually key to that because by sharing content you get people to come to your profile.

Adam Ashton: Yeah.

Chris J. Reed: By putting the right keywords in, you get found on a search, and they come to your profile. If they access your brand first, it's much easier for you to then approach them and say, 'Thank you for viewing my profile, thanks for commenting, thanks for sharing my blog. Now, do you want to have a chat about LinkedIn? Because they've already started accessing my brand, they're much more likely to say yes than if you just reach out to them cold through an email or a phone call, for example, where they don't know you from Adam.

Adam Ashton: Yeah.

Chris J. Reed: Basically, LinkedIn; they know who you are.

Adam Ashton: Yeah, very nice, and the other reason you said LinkedIn is far superior to FaceBook, especially for business-to-business is that on LinkedIn it's there for business. FaceBook, not so much.

Chris J. Reed: Yeah, it's the data. It's basically the data. The data overwhelmingly on LinkedIn is phenomenal. Whereas, on FaceBook, you don't say where you work, you don't say where you used to work, you don't say where you went to school, you don't see your connections, or people you both know, in a business context. Well, with LinkedIn you do, and that's part of it.

If you connect with someone or message someone, the first thing they can do is, they can check out the hundred people you both know together. Then, there's reference points. If they can see your content marketing strategy in a business context, there are reference points. If they can see you went to the same university, or the same company five years ago, 10 years ago, there are reference points, and that's so you know LinkedIn and business is all about relationship-building and relationships. Just like anything in life, it's about relationships, but in a business context.

The more personal references, the more joint references and shared references you both have, the more chance somebody will say yes to you. That's all about building up your entire profile on LinkedIn to give people more hooks and more reasons to say yes than if they don't know who you are.

Adam Ashton: Mm-hmm (affirmative). For sure. That's awesome. The other thing you mentioned before and I sort of skipped over because I wanted to come back to it later was, you mentioned company pages. Again, this is something available to everyone?

Chris J. Reed: Yes, it is, but it's phenomenally hard to actually do it very well. I'll give you a quick example. Richard Branson has the number one followed profile on LinkedIn, with 13 million followers. Virgin Atlantic has a hundred thousand. That's less than 1%.

Richard Branson has the holistically positive effect over the entire Virgin brands because of things like his blogging or that he never mentions things, like the individual Virgin brands. People like to back up his companies, or anybody's companies, by having a company page there because you do get found and get on Google.

If I google my company, Black Marketing, the second thing that comes up is my LinkedIn company page. Point of reference there, people can see what we're sharing about LinkedIn on there, and people can see how many employees we have and so forth. It's very important in terms of an employer branding point of view. They can see you.

Also, on the app, as we discussed before, people don't like leaving the app, so they can check out your company page on the app, they're reassured that you're a proper company; whereas if you don't put your company on, you look like a one-man band.

Adam Ashton: For sure.

Chris J. Reed: Therefore, you lose credibility and you can charge less as a result. People like to know that they're dealing with a company rather than a sole trader.

Adam Ashton: Yeah. Absolutely. Yeah, and as you say, they don't want to have to go from LinkedIn on their phone, open up an Internet app, and then find your website.

Chris J. Reed: That's right. They're just not going to do it.

Adam Ashton: Cool. You mentioned sharing, so what sort of stuff should your company page be sharing?

Chris J. Reed: Your company page is slightly different from your personal page in that you should be sharing things about your company and about services and about your profession . . . Basically, what your company actually does. We take the view that we don't just share about Black Marketing, we share about everything to do with LinkedIn. Then, it becomes a centre of excellence for everything about LinkedIn. I don't care if one of our competitors wrote it. If it's relevant about LinkedIn, I'll share it.

If it's LinkedIn stuff, I'll share it. If it's videos, I'll share it. If it's info graphics, I'll share it. If it's anything to do with LinkedIn or content marketing or social selling, I'll put it on my LinkedIn, and then I'll probably share it with every single one of my followers who can actually see it as well, but it has come from my company page first.

Adam Ashton: Nice.

Chris J. Reed: Whereas on my page, I'll share stuff that's not about LinkedIn. I'll follow the 4-1-1 rule much more readily. Whereas, on the company page, you can get away with the fact that it should be about your services but not just about your company. That's where I make the distinction there. I don't just share things about Black Marketing, I share things about LinkedIn.

Adam Ashton: Yeah. Yeah, cool.

Chris J. Reed: It can be about other people talking about LinkedIn and how they use LinkedIn, but it's all about LinkedIn, whether it's about Black Marketing or my events, or whether it's about just being the best way of using LinkedIn from a *Forbes* article or *Wall Street Journal* article or *FD* article or *The Australian* article. It's about LinkedIn, and it's a channel if you want to know anything about LinkedIn: up to date about the new LinkedIn, for example. It's all on the Black Marketing page.

Adam Ashton: Very nice. Very nice and, the other thing, which I had no idea, I haven't made a company page, but until I read your book, the showcase pages. What's the go there? Because I've never heard of it.

Chris J. Reed: Yeah. It's one of these LinkedIn things that LinkedIn didn't bother telling anyone about. Basically, showcase pages are like website tabs. You know, on a website you have About Us, Services, Case Studies, Contact Us. LinkedIn enabled you to have showcase pages that do the same thing. What you should use it for is optimisation. If you look at Sheila Packard's page, for example, it's a very good way to do this.

There you have Sheila Packard on the front page. Then their showcase page is like Hewitt Packard Labs, Hewitt Packard Graphics, Hewitt

Packard Printing, Hewitt Packard Enterprise. All of their divisions then have a page, and that means, if you're sharing things about HP Graphics, the branding that comes up is HP Graphics, not HP.

It's a distinction. We have things like personal branding as a page.

Adam Ashton: Nice.

Chris J. Reed: Content marketing is a page. Thought leadership is a page. Social selling is a page. Lead generation is a page. Company branding is a page, but all of them say, 'Powered by Black Marketing'. If you do a search, for example, on personal branding, our company showcase page comes up.

Adam Ashton: Mm-hmm (affirmative). Nice.

Chris J. Reed: It's all about optimising it for LinkedIn. It also means if someone comes to my page, a bit like a website, they can then go to individual areas and learn about the different things we do through the content we share on the showcase pages.

Adam Ashton: Fantastic. OK, that sounds good. Something I need to look into.

Chris J. Reed: I mean, it's free as well. It's all free.

Adam Ashton: Yeah, exactly. OK, so I think one last LinkedIn question, before we shift gears, is the messaging. What are people doing wrong? What should we be doing? What are people missing in terms of messaging?

Chris J. Reed: The biggest thing that people do wrong is they try and basically sell their entire company on a message. They basically put down all the things they do, even before they've even met somebody, and you see reams of paper coming towards you. Oh, my God. Whereas, what we do is we believe in the three-line rule, which is saying, this is what we do, this is what we can do for you, I'd like to meet you. That's it.

Adam Ashton: Nice.

Chris J. Reed: And that works.

Adam Ashton: Nice.

Chris J. Reed: The simple and short is better. For example, my meetings last week in Melbourne had the headline of visiting Melbourne. The first line said, 'I'm visiting Melbourne and I'd like to talk to you about your LinkedIn marketing strategy'. My second line was, 'When are you free?' That was it, and then my signature said, 'Chris Reed and NASDAQ-listed company, author, power profiler', all the rest of it, but that was it.

Adam Ashton: Yeah, nice.

Chris J. Reed: People appreciated the fact that they're busy people; I appreciated the fact that they're busy people. Basically, it was a simple question. They could see my profile, they could see my headline, they could see what I do. If they wanted to do LinkedIn, they would say yes. That's why it worked because we appreciated their time, so the simple is always better. LinkedIn basically says that the shorter the message, the more response you will actually get. You're basically shooting yourself in the foot if you're elongating it. You're never ever going to sell someone on LinkedIn.

Adam Ashton: Yeah, for sure.

Chris J. Reed: What you want to do is have a meeting. You want to basically say to everyone, 'This is what we do, let's have a meeting, and then talk about it'. Then, if you close them as a result of that, fantastic. If you don't, then so be it, but you're never going to close them on LinkedIn. People make that mistake; they're just going to pick up the pace to do that. Someone's never going to say, 'Yes, I want to buy your product for a million dollars', straightaway. It's not going to happen.

Adam Ashton: Yeah.

Chris J. Reed: They have to meet. Again, it goes back to social selling. It's all about you.

Adam Ashton: Yeah.

Chris J. Reed: They're buying you, but they have to meet you, whether it's a Skype or a phone call or an actual physical meeting. That's why I do so many meetings in different countries. That's why I went to Melbourne last week because I know I can close my deals face-to-face.

Adam Ashton: Yeah, absolutely.

Chris J. Reed: Then I can do over the telephone or Skype, and never just by having a conversation on email. It's not going to happen. It's all about personal relationships.

Adam Ashton: Yeah, fantastic and the other thing you said in the book is that you always get notifications, 'Such and such viewed your profile and you should message them' . . . What should we say when we get that notification?

Chris J. Reed: As soon as you get that, you should say, 'Thank you for viewing my profile', so be polite. With every single interaction on LinkedIn, you should always say thank you. 'Thank you for commenting on this. Thank you for sharing. Thank you for liking', and then ask, 'Would you like to talk about your LinkedIn marketing strategy?' whatever your service happens to be. Because they viewed your profile, they will normally fire back and say, 'Oh, yes, you came up in a search or as someone who would do my LinkedIn', or they'll say, 'I got recommended to you by somebody else', or they'll say, 'I read your article in one of my publications' or 'I was curious about your profile'.

Whichever way, you acknowledge them.

Adam Ashton: Yeah.

Chris J. Reed: People like to be acknowledged. It's just human nature. People like to be noticed; somebody asked what they did, was noticed by somebody else. It's just simple little things on LinkedIn, which if you do well, it's part of the whole social selling ethos. I'm just noticing, saying hello, saying thank you; just saying thank you works amazingly well on LinkedIn.

Adam Ashton: Yeah. Nice. As I was reading that, and even as you're saying it now, there is some kind of discomfort within me, thinking, I would definitely hold back. It sounds obvious. Someone views your profile, they're obviously somewhat interested.

Chris J. Reed: Correct.

Adam Ashton: Then, I'm already holding back thinking I wouldn't want to message them. What's that about?

Chris J. Reed: That's what I call being English. English people have a problem in terms of modesty. The problem with modesty on LinkedIn is that you will get some American to come along who will basically claim they've done something, even when they haven't, as being proved by, obviously, the current United States president.

They will actually say, 'I invented the earth'. You go, 'No, you didn't'. 'No, I did. Here's my LinkedIn references to say so'. 'Oh, well, you must have invented the earth. I'll go with it'. Well, actually the real guy was living in Melbourne; he just didn't put it on his LinkedIn.

Modesty gets you nowhere on LinkedIn. You have to be proactive because they do give you all the data. LinkedIn says that you can do this. LinkedIn says publish, LinkedIn says you can share, LinkedIn says here's your company page, LinkedIn says put your recommendations down. LinkedIn says you can do the awards, and LinkedIn says this person viewed your profile.

It's up to you whether you want to follow up or not. A lot of people don't do it, which is where we come in, because we say you need to be proactive as well as reactive, but you could be missing out on millions of dollars' worth of contracts because they've viewed your profile because they're interested in your services. Then, you basically don't follow up, then you're missing out. They're not missing out. They'll find somebody else to do it. Then you're missing out. You're missing out on that golden opportunity.

Adam Ashton: Yeah, nice.

Chris J. Reed: Last thing: They should be more American about it.

Adam Ashton: Yeah, exactly. Love it. There's one more thing that I was going to say, the Sales Navigator, obviously, I've listened to about six or eight of your past podcast interviews in preparation for this, so I knew of Sales Navigator. Before listening to those, I was pretty much unaware of Sales Navigator. Can you give us a quick description, and why we should use it?

Chris J. Reed: Sure. It's basically another secret jam that LinkedIn didn't really market very well. Sales Navigator is the sales and marketing platform of LinkedIn. It allows you to find anyone anywhere in the world using search criteria, and the search is very, very good because it goes down to . . . I can find, like last week in Melbourne, I can find CEOs of companies 10 to 11 to 500 size. Then, I can go even further down and say, 'OK, these people have to have experience of at least 10 years, they have to have been on LinkedIn for at least five years'.

I can put all of this criteria down. I also then looked even deeper and said these people have to have posted on LinkedIn and in the last 30 days. Now that rules out about two-thirds of the world's population.

Adam Ashton: Yeah.

Chris J. Reed: When it comes to LinkedIn, only about one in four, one in three people are actually active on LinkedIn at any one moment. Obviously, if you want to message somebody using Sales Navigator, you want them to respond. If they're not active on LinkedIn, they're not going to respond. It does not matter how good your profile is or how good your message is, if they're not using it, they are not going to see it.

Adam Ashton: Yeah.

Chris J. Reed: Using the data on Sales Navigator allows you to find the right person but also find that they're actually active. Then you send a nice message, and you can track the messaging as well. It allows you to build a target list. So, last week when I was in Melbourne, I had this massive list, this target list. I connected with people, which enabled me to have more target lists because of the way LinkedIn works. That

185

is, if I connect with you, I get access to your first connections, which become my second connections, and their first connections become my third connections.

Every time I connect with a new entrepreneur in Melbourne, I broaden my database of potential leads and that's absolutely crucial because Sales Navigator then tells me that and I can build up more data on Sales Navigator to find more people and you build entire pipelines because of it, because the more people you connect with, the right kind of people . . . CEOs tend to know other CEOs.

Adam Ashton: Yeah.

Chris J. Reed: You build up your portfolio, but only Sales Navigator can tell you who changed jobs, who's active on LinkedIn, and who's in the news recently. With all three of these things, you can personalise a message as a result of it. Only Sales Navigator can do that for you.

Adam Ashton: Fantastic, and that's the paid Premium versions, though. Right?

Chris J. Reed: It's the paid Premium version, but it's the same cost as Recruiter Lite and the same cost as Premium itself. It just gives you more data, so if you're in the lead generation business, or even if you just want to find investors or PR people . . .

Adam Ashton: Yeah.

Chris J. Reed: Employees. Actually, Sales Navigator allows you to do all those things. It just allows you to find anybody on LinkedIn, for whatever reason you want to. It's good for investors. If you want to find investors, you could find investors by putting in things like 'angel investor' or 'VC' into the keywords. A lot of people are active on LinkedIn who invest in Star-tips or invest in technology or invest in Melbourne or invest in Victoria. You can find that using LinkedIn Sales Navigator.

Adam Ashton: Awesome.

Chris J. Reed: You use it for whatever you want to do, but clients; we use it mostly to find clients.

Adam Ashton: Yeah. Fantastic. Man, you've given us so much valuable LinkedIn stuff, and there's definitely some tweaks I need to make after this. You said you're the number one profile. Is that in Australia and Singapore or in a few other countries?

Chris J. Reed: Views.

Adam Ashton: Views.

Chris J. Reed: Purely views.

Adam Ashton: Yeah.

Chris J. Reed: Followers are well up there, but the trouble with followers is you can get somebody like an MD of a bank, like Mike Smith at ANZ, for example.

Adam Ashton: Yeah.

Chris J. Reed: Or Piyush Gupta at DBS. They don't actually use it, and also they haven't actually done it.

Adam Ashton: Yeah.

Chris J. Reed: They'd be put on there because it's part of their corporate coms, but they're not actually using it, and you can tell they're not actually using it because they blog like every half a year.

Adam Ashton: Yeah, exactly.

Chris J. Reed: And they share something every five years, or something like that, so it's not real people. You can't really judge it by followers; you judge it by engagement. I have the most amount of views in Singapore and Australia, and my social selling index is number one in Singapore and Australia as well.

Adam Ashton: Yeah.

Chris J. Reed: That's how we basically judge it. Unfortunately, LinkedIn took away the rankings when they did the new LinkedIn, so you now can't actually tell where you are amongst professionals like you or your company or other things, but I know in the last set of rankings I had I was beating, for example, the managing director of LinkedIn in Asia Pacific, which is always a good thing to do if you beat the managing director of LinkedIn. He runs the platform.

Adam Ashton: You're doing something right. That's for sure.

Chris J. Reed: Doing something right, yes. Basically, that's how we know how we're doing. Also, this guy at LinkedIn in Australia actually told me I had number one, in terms of social selling index and number of views as well.

Adam Ashton: Fantastic.

Chris J. Reed: That's why he was interested in what we could actually do for them as well.

Adam Ashton: Fantastic. I know we're sort of running out of time, but I just wanted to quickly ask you a few things about the book itself. *LinkedIn Mastery for Entrepreneurs*, you said it's the number one LinkedIn book.

Chris J. Reed: Yep.

Adam Ashton: Out of 55,000 LinkedIn books on Amazon.

Chris J. Reed: On LinkedIn, there's only so much you can do, and people say to me, 'Is there anything else you can tell us about LinkedIn?' I say, 'Well, not really, because that's it. It's a closed platform. There's only so much you can do'. You can't suddenly start painting pictures. You just can't do other things.

You can't make any vegetables on it. There's nothing much you can do. It's a platform, you have certain things you can do, some things you can't do, and you have to use it for what you can actually do, which is the personal branding, the employee branding, the social selling, and the content marketing, and that's it.

Adam Ashton: Yeah.

Chris J. Reed: If you do these things and you fill out all the details, then your standard rank, your rankings will be better.

Chris J. Reed: Even if 95% of the people listening here never become my clients, they'll all tell other people about it: 'I heard a great guy talk about LinkedIn, he does this, he does that, he has a Mohawk', and so forth. People go away from my talks, like in Melbourne last week I did four talks, and every single person went away from those talks raving about what we did.

Adam Ashton: Yeah.

Chris J. Reed: What we do and the Mohawk, and taking pictures, and I shared on LinkedIn and they shared on LinkedIn, for example. It's all about using LinkedIn to basically give away content, using my book, using my talks, using my blogs, and using podcasts to give away content. The people then have a look at LinkedIn and say, 'This is too difficult. I can't do this myself. I need to outsource it to Chris. I won't do it myself, and I'll thank Black Marketing and Chris Reed because of it'.

Adam Ashton: Yeah.

Chris J. Reed: That just gives us a massive amount of PR. You have to be willing to be completely holistic about it and not be precious.

Adam Ashton: Yeah, nice.

Chris J. Reed: Because if you're precious and you think you can make money out of selling some information that other people don't know about, you're not going to make any money at all. You'll waste years of your life trying to do it. Whereas, I firmly believe in giving away content, and people say to me, 'You're giving away all of your secrets in the book', and I go, 'Yeah'.

I'm quite happy for anybody to follow this and people say, 'What happens if somebody else sets up a company to rival you, and do the same thing?' I say, 'Good luck', because basically I employ 25 people, and it's very labour-intensive.

Adam Ashton: Yeah, exactly.

Chris J. Reed: I work 24/7, and I spend a lot of time on LinkedIn learning about what you do, what not to do, and it's very hard because it's not an exact science. I'll give you a good example. The blogging is a good example. I can write a blog, which I've spent hours on, days on, researching, and it'll get a couple hundred people viewing it, no one liking, no one sharing, no one commenting.

Then, I'll write one in like half an hour, on a whim, about something I don't really care about, put it out there, and then it goes viral.

Adam Ashton: Yeah.

Chris J. Reed: Get like tens of thousands of people coming to you . . . How did that even happen? The same thing when it comes to new businesses. You can have everything lined up and think that a city, maybe like New York or somewhere, is going to get you lots of leads, and it doesn't. Then you go somewhere like Melbourne, and it does get you lots of leads and you go, 'Well, that's interesting. I would have thought it's the other way around'.

You just learn about human nature, you learn about business, and basically all you can do is set up LinkedIn so that it helps you build your business and do your business in the right kind of way. That's how I approach the book. The book is basically for every single person to go away and do it for themselves, just like my talks. You come to my talk and you can take away all the tips and do it yourself.

Adam Ashton: Yeah.

Chris J. Reed: If you really want to, you can employ us, but you don't have to. That's the whole point. That's why I get invited to so many talks because I'm not trying to sell my company, because I'm trying to sell the ability, the benefit to you from doing LinkedIn.

Adam Ashton: Yeah.

Chris J. Reed: It's all about you. Ultimately, it's all about you. LinkedIn's about you. It's not about Black Marketing or about me or about you. It's about you, as in you are the individual, which will benefit the most by investing in LinkedIn. It's your personal brand. Ultimately, your personal brand will stay with you for the rest of your life, and it's up to you to invest in it.

Adam Ashton: Fantastic and I liked what you said about giving the book away, instead of the business card, because it's . . . I don't know, I just sent my book to the printers and I don't know how thick yours is, because I read it on the Kindle, but it was less than two dollars a book to print and so much more effective.

Chris J. Reed: Precisely.

Adam Ashton: People will look at a business card and throw it away.

Chris J. Reed: Precisely, precisely.

Adam Ashton: Whereas a book, they've got it.

Chris J. Reed: Precisely, it'll be on their bookshelf and it will be on their desk, and they'll recommend it to other people and they'll share it with other people. Believe me, I've had so many people say to me, 'I've read the book or I was passed your book by somebody else or I've heard your audio book or I've read it on the Kindle', or whatever and it's just, that's phenomenal.

Adam Ashton: Yeah.

Chris J. Reed: That you've actually given something back to somebody that's actually managed to change their lives or they've thought about something because you've challenged them and you've actually stimulated the thought. That's amazing.

Adam Ashton: Yeah and it's super cheap on Amazon as well. If I learn about the background picture and put that up, I'd say that's worth the couple of bucks I spent on the book. That's for sure.

Chris J. Reed: Yeah and the audiobook is free on Amazon, at the moment, because we're doing a promotion. The audiobook is really good as well.

Adam Ashton: Awesome. Can you tell us about your programme? What do you do for those upper-echelon clients?

Chris J. Reed: Well, I wouldn't describe them as upper-echelon clients. I say it's expensive because I get told by people it's expensive, and we deliberately put it as Premium. We charge between three and five thousand dollars a month, for example. To do that, we have four people on your account, so we have one person who will write your blogs, so they're in effect, the editor. They will go to write your blogs and then publish it.

We have an account manager who will actually amplify the blogs because it's not just about writing it, you have to across people to make sure people read it and see it, answer comments, answer links, optimise your profile, put the background picture up, put your headline up, put a picture up, a summary section, add your weblinks in, add your videos in, add your YouTube in, add your infographics in.

We make sure your profile looks very visual, very happening, and maybe not just words, but lots of visual from your website, for example. Then, we'll have somebody who does the Sales Navigator. That's a real specialist. I mean, you have to know how to really use Sales Navigator to get the most out of it. We have a team of people at Black Marketing in Singapore who just work on Sales Navigator, and then we have an account director overseeing everything to make sure that all the stats are coming through as well. Plus, I look at it every single week as well. You get five people on your accounts, so three and a half thousand, $4,000 a month.

Adam Ashton: Yeah.

Chris J. Reed: Now, if you could find someone in Australia, including superannuation, bearing in mind that you have to pay them holiday pay and sick pay and superannuation, they won't know how to write a blog.

Adam Ashton: Yeah.

Chris J. Reed: You need to do Sales Navigator and account manage LinkedIn at the same time because those are different skill sets.

Adam Ashton: Yeah.

Chris J. Reed: Especially if you have to employ three people, so eventually, you end up paying about $15,000.

Adam Ashton: Yeah.

Chris J. Reed: Whereas, you could just outsource it to us. Plus, one of the reasons why I invest so much into things like the book is, I'm a power profiler in Singapore and have been for five years running. I am the number one profile in Singapore and Australia, so basically if you want someone who's an expert to look after your LinkedIn profile, you would come to me. There are lots of people out there in Melbourne, for example, and also in Australia, who are trainers on LinkedIn, but the first thing you have to do is look at their profiles.

You look at their profiles: If they've already got a couple of thousand connections, it might sound like a lot, but look at mine. I've got 55,000 and I've got the book and I've got the company, indexing, obviously, on NASDAQ, and the book and the Power Profile and lots of other awards as well, and you have to really look at who you want looking after your LinkedIn profile.

Adam Ashton: Exactly. Yeah.

Chris J. Reed: You can always go cheap, but ultimately you get what you pay for.

Adam Ashton: Exactly. I think I'd go with the Mohawk, for sure. With the NASDAQ company, with the book, the number one LinkedIn book, absolutely, so how can people find out more about Chris Reed? I'd say if they type 'Chris Reed', R double E, D into LinkedIn, they'll probably find you?

Chris J. Reed: Yeah, or even Google, obviously.

Adam Ashton: Yeah, exactly. Love it.

Chris J. Reed: 'Chris J. Reed Mohawk' into Google. 'Chris J. Reed Singapore' into Google. Just 'Chris J. Reed' normally, LinkedIn. It comes up, obviously, number one in Google as well in Australia. I tested it last week in Melbourne. It works in Melbourne. It works in Sydney.

Adam Ashton: Yeah, nice.

Chris J. Reed: It works in Adelaide. It works in Brisbane. It works in Canberra. It works across the whole of Australia as well as Hong Kong and Singapore and everywhere else.

Adam Ashton: Fantastic. Well, thank you very much for that, Chris Reed. I learned so much, and I've written down a whole bunch of notes that I need to go away and fix about my LinkedIn profile. Is there anything you want to leave us with?

Chris J. Reed: Just get on LinkedIn and get stuck into it.

Adam Ashton: Get on there.

Chris J. Reed: 'Cause the more you do it, the more benefit you'll get. It's a good education platform. Literally, the more you do, the more you'll benefit from it. Your rankings will rise immediately, so just get stuck into LinkedIn.

Adam Ashton: Fantastic. Thank you very much, Chris, and all the best on the next leg of the world tour.

Chris J. Reed: Pleasure.

Adam Ashton: Cheers.

Chapter Twenty-Five

What Is The Dark Art of Marketing?

Personal Branding for Entrepreneurs

The Dark Art of Marketing—Personal Branding for Entrepreneurs will transform your personal brand to rock-star status and is led by multi-award-winning LinkedIn Power Profile, NASDAQ CEO, and #1 international best-selling author Chris J. Reed. Our highly exclusive boutique personal branding consultancy will manage all aspects of your personal brand.

We will manage your LinkedIn profile to your YouTube channel, from your interviews and blogs to your speaking engagements and award entries, networking at the right events and the way you look and dress. The Dark Art of Marketing will intelligently ensure that your personal brand is one to be reckoned with, using both sophistication and panache.

Chris will create and design an advanced strategy that elevates your personal brand and will implement your ideal personal branding strategy, as well as achieve your personal professional objectives.

Chris will personally manage this process to ensure true quality in execution and communications. For this highly sought-after, highly personal service, Chris will only be accepting a limited number of clients at a negotiable rate, depending on the amount of advanced and enhanced personal branding that you desire.

Chris will personally manage this process to ensure true quality in execution and communications. Contact Chris, and let's start your personal branding journey via a free consultation.

Visit Chris's website for more information:
http://www.thedarkartofmarketing.com

Endorsements

Veronika Bilkova
Entrepreneur; Founder; Managing Director at EFTLab of Smarter Payment Solutions.

It was a very inspiring workshop. If you would like to boost your LinkedIn profile and know more about content-driven marketing, you should definitely attend one of his sessions.

Sarah Crundall
CEO Premium Skincare; Team Mentor; Transforming Leadership & Culture; Brand Coach; #1 PREMIUM Skincare; Rodan and Fields.

Wow, WOW, wow! It was a fantastic power session that Chris held. If you would like a really comprehensive, fast, and in-depth education on the ins and outs of LinkedIn, then I would highly recommend you connect with Chris. The session was so jam-packed with energy and information. I was thrilled that I decided to book in. If you're in doubt, definitely check it out. Thanks, Chris and your Mohawk.

Brian Clark
Sales Productivity; Execution Performance Consultant for IT, Software, and Professional Services Companies.

The workshop was filled with energy, passion, and information that was expertly communicated by Chris. I am so impressed by the amount of insights, tips, and tools that were included. I have learned so much and left the session with a buzz to get to work on my LinkedIn profile. I am so fortunate to have connected with Chris, and I recommend him without hesitation.

Paul J. McCarrison
CEO, Director, and Entrepreneur—Partnering with Entrepreneurs and Brand Challengers for Awesome Digital Marketing and Growth.

After having read Chris's book, and having consulted with him, we implemented his recommendations in our own direct marketing processes, and I am pleased to say that his lessons have been invaluable. Within the first week, we picked up our first client via LinkedIn using his methodology. We absolutely see the value in what he offers and are looking forward to the results on the horizon as a result of his teachings. It is definitely worth investing in Chris's time.

Adrian Keane
Founder and Chief Executive at Edify; Global Rights; Educational Technology; Book Publishing; Curriculum Resources.

Had the very good fortune to attend Chris's seminar on succeeding with LinkedIn. Chris is an engaging presenter, very knowledgeable, and good fun. The time flies by as he shines a light on the substantial opportunities that exist through the LinkedIn platform. He has got a mint Mohawk, and he is a snappy dresser. If you get the chance to attend a workshop, then do yourself a favour and get there. So many executives and companies, large and small, are completely missing the action on LinkedIn; don't be one of them. Chris can help!

Kirsten Taylor
Managing Director of SleepDrops International Limited.

Chris certainly knows his stuff when it comes to LinkedIn! His presentation was not only interesting, but also entertaining. He gave the entire room a lot of practical advice, and we all left the room with some great ideas on how to better make use of this powerful business tool and harness the motivation to do so. I will be updating my page very soon. No doubt, you'll get notified. Thanks, Chris.

Scott Freeman
Connecting Senior and Future Leaders to Great Companies.

If you think you have LinkedIn covered and have not yet heard Chris talk, think again! Full of enthusiasm, insight, and great advice, he'll improve your online profile and your ability to generate leads and develop business relationships.

Neil James

I help organisations adapt and grow in line with changing markets. Key Skills: Sales, Commercial, Change IT, Coaching.

I thoroughly recommend making the time to connect with Chris and attend one of his events. The content is memorable and provocative (in a positive way!), and leaves you with no choice but to take action. If you cannot attend an event, purchase a copy of his book. It's worth the investment.

Susan Toby
Conversations That Matter; CEO of Conversations That Matter Specialist; Consultant; Coach; Counsellor Training; Change Enabler.

Standing out from the crowd with his Mohawk and red-coloured shoes, Chris's energetic, fast-paced workshop is full of valuable content. Though I have been using LinkedIn for many years, the evolution of the new platform meant that I had much to learn, and I found it useful and certainly value for money. Thank you, Chris, for a great workshop. It's a workshop that I would highly recommend to anyone working in their own business or marketing for another company.

Jacqueline A. Low
COO at Hawsford, Singapore Pty Ltd.

I attended an animated and insightful talk by Chris yesterday, and took away some very important intelligence that I can use to improve. I didn't realise how the little things can make a difference until Chris highlighted them. I will be using what I have learned. Thanks, Chris!

Vincent Kelly
Co-Founder at Frau Zogg Pty Ltd.

I thought I had a good grip on LinkedIn, but that was before I went to one of Chris J. Rockstar's seminars. In 2.5 hours, I had my world of connectivity turned upside-down. A word of warning though—you will learn so much that you might be slightly overwhelmed with all of the new information. That's OK though because you can always engage Chris and his team to run LinkedIn for you, which is what I will be doing. Even if you don't, you will walk away with enough information so that you will be performing 100% better on the platform. There is nothing like LinkedIn for business and peer-to-peer connectivity, and there is no one like Chris J. Rockstar to help you get the best out of it!

Brad Smith

My digital marketing expertise, business acumen, and entrepreneurial approach create tangible growth across any industry.

I recently attended Black Marketing's Enabling LinkedIn For You course, taught by Chris Reed. What an amazing course and very insightful. I highly recommend this course to anyone who wants to advance their knowledge and skills on LinkedIn. Chris is well-connected, and he is a very passionate LinkedIn professional who has an in-depth understanding about how LinkedIn works. He strives to be the very best in his professional undertakings.